Power Up Power Down

"By treating the critical role of power in the workplace informatively, engagingly, and insightfully, Gail Rudolph has given each of us a valuable gift that will keep on giving from the present well into the future."

—**Robert B. Cialdini, PhD**, *New York Times* Best Selling Author, *Influence* and *Pre-Suasion*

"Gail Rudolph has a vast understanding of power, and she knows how to utilize that understanding to create win/win opportunities for everyone involved. It is wonderful that she is now making her expertise available in *Power Up Power Down*! In this book, you can experience Gail's style, feel her virtual smile, and sense her ability to explain power in a way that can help us all make the shift to embrace our personal empowerment to become an agent of influence and change. I highly recommend you grab this book and start reading—it truly has the power to change your life as you grasp what it means to Power Up and Power Down."

—**Tim Enochs**, *New York Times* Best Selling Author, President and Founder of NEWLife Leadership

"For those who have struggled with accessing personal power, *Power Up Power Down* clears a pathway of understanding, creating the internal shift needed to harness power properly for the good of all involved. As an organizational psychologist who consults with people, teams, and organizations to lead successful and sustainable change, I know how vital it is to approach any transformation from the inside out. Gail shines a spotlight on the areas that keep us from being able to appropriately and effectively use the power we all possess."

—**Barbara A. Trautlein, PhD**, Best Selling Author, *Change Intelligence*, Chief Catalyst at Change Catalysts

"Power is wielded in positive and negative ways, and its impact is undeniable. In *Power Up Power Down*, Gail unpacks the role that power plays in our professional interactions and careers and then equips us to better understand, and wisely leverage, power dynamics. By clearly identifying the situations where power is often misused, Gail effectively teaches us how to use the concepts of power up and power down to create a successful outcome—even in the most difficult situations."

—**Susie Albert Miller, MA, MDiv,** Best Selling Author
Listen, Learn, Love

"For someone whose job is to help people resolve problems and make headway toward better living in our city, Gail's book is an invaluable resource. The stories in *Power Up Power Down* are captivating and intriguing; many resonated with me as they shed light on power situations I've personally encountered. After reading Gail's book, I am even more aware of how vital it is to understand that we all have power and influence. Knowing how to step into the right role thoughtfully and with purpose is essential, and *Power Up Power Down* hands us the key to unlock the door to personal empowerment and help others do the same. We can all become better citizens wherever we live by reading *Power Up Power Down*."

—**Diane Howard,** Mayor, Redwood City, CA

"It is absolutely necessary for women to understand how they are showing up in order to be successful! We must equip ourselves with the tools needed to respond to any situation. "Understanding our power and the energy of others is so important to being an effective communicator.

Gail shows us in *Power Up Power Down* how to be prepared for any situation by respecting others and understanding the energy in a room. We all have choices about how we respond to challenges; Gail shows us how to do that effectively."

—**Charli K. Matthews**, Empowering Women in Industry

"*Power Up Power Down* should be required reading for every med school student and every practicing medical professional—especially physicians. Thought-provoking and candid, Gail brings to light a topic that is often taboo in the medical world. Well done, Gail!"

—**Linda Dew, MD, FRCPC**

"I often say that the most important skill to develop is influence. In *Power Up Power Down*, Gail demonstrates powerful techniques packed with enriching stories that show why it is important to develop this key skill. Gail shows deceptively simple techniques to overcome negative self-talk, set boundaries, and how to deal with a Negatron, along with delightfully memorable power tools. All of this great advice is woven in with a keen understanding of communication styles to ensure that the messages can be delivered effectively."

—**Rick A. Morris**, Best Selling Author and Executive Director, John Maxwell Team President, R2 Consulting

"Other educators and I have often noted that children wield and use power from their earliest days, whether it's in the front of the class or on the playground. After reading *Power Up Power Down*, it became clear that the classroom is the perfect place to teach what it means to Power Up or Power Down. The ideas and strategies Gail has laid out will help my students understand power dynamics and help them discover ways they can become more aware of themselves and more sensitive to other children. And hopefully, one day, they will become more aware and more sensitive adults. Thank you, Gail—this is a book every teacher needs to read!"

—Jenny Scott, Special Education Teacher
Licensed Learning Behavior Specialist

"Gail weaves the concept of personal leadership through every chapter, demonstrating the influence personal power can have in the hands of an exceptional leader. Her book brings to life how important it is to intentionally choose everything we think, say, and do if we want to achieve lasting impact in our life, love, and leadership. A 'grow your people' playbook for both emerging and established leaders in any industry."

—Ann Vertel, PhD, Business Psychologist
Leadership Consultant

POWER UP POWER DOWN

How to Reclaim Control and Make Every Situation a Win/Win

GAIL RUDOLPH

NEW YORK

LONDON • NASHVILLE • MELBOURNE • VANCOUVER

POWER UP POWER DOWN

How to Reclaim Control and Make Every Situation a Win/Win

Published in New York, New York, by Morgan James Publishing. Morgan James is a trademark of Morgan James, LLC. www.MorganJamesPublishing.com

Morgan James BOGO™

A **FREE** ebook edition is available for you or a friend with the purchase of this print book.

CLEARLY SIGN YOUR NAME ABOVE

Instructions to claim your free ebook edition:
1. Visit MorganJamesBOGO.com
2. Sign your name CLEARLY in the space above
3. Complete the form and submit a photo of this entire page
4. You or your friend can download the ebook to your preferred device

ISBN 9781631955068 paperback
ISBN 9781631955075 ebook
Library of Congress Control Number:
2021930917

Cover Design by:
Jason Clement
www.jasonclement.com

Interior Design by:
Chris Treccani
www.3dogcreative.net

Author Photo by:
Mike Lloyd
www.mikelloydphoto.com

Morgan James is a proud partner of Habitat for Humanity Peninsula and Greater Williamsburg. Partners in building since 2006.

Get involved today! Visit
MorganJamesPublishing.com/giving-back

To the two people who continue to amaze me, my children, Josephine and Andrew.

Throughout the months of writing this book, you have been my sounding board, encouragers, and best of friends. Thank you for being my biggest supporters, even in the midst of separately moving across the country to pursue your own dreams.

You are both becoming incredible examples of influence. I am blessed and honored to be your mother!

TABLE OF CONTENTS

FOREWORD

Some years ago, before getting into the book business and eventually becoming a book coach and author, I worked as a Marriage and Family Therapist.

As a clinician, it was easy to see how power played out in relationships—between couples, parents, children, and siblings. When working with families, I could see who was using power to their advantage and who was not using power, occasionally to their disadvantage. Sometimes I could see that the kids were running the show; sometimes the balance of power in couples was clearly way off-kilter. And sometimes, there were power plays with long-lasting impact from people who weren't even in the room.

I often saw that families had the most trouble when those power undercurrents went unaddressed. Although it was painful to explore, I knew we had to address those power issues in strategic ways if we wanted to achieve better, healthier, and more enjoyable relationships.

The lessons and observations I learned as a therapist have stuck with me over time as I've navigated the business world. The corporate arena is less shy about admitting the role of power; in fact, "power moves" and "power players" are often embraced and celebrated. But there seemed to be a void when it came to actually addressing the "elephant in the room"—the unique ways in which women in corporate America can and should use power.

That's why I couldn't have been more pleased when I was introduced to Gail Rudolph by a mutual friend. As a corporate consultant and highly skilled trainer, Gail talks about many of the same power issues I observed in a clinical setting—but she tackles those issues in the work setting.

What I love about Gail is that she has made it her passion and life's work to shine a light on how power plays out in the workplace. She reveals many of the power dynamics that we experience every day but don't pay much attention to—even though those dynamics often impact our work in challenging ways (and frequently spill over at home).

Power is part of all our relationships. It is fluid and plays out in subtle and, often, not so subtle ways. But as Gail explains, power isn't just something that "happens to us." Power is a choice and a tool—and Gail is a master at looking at, and working on, power *intentionally*.

So, can we use, and even leverage, that power? Gail answers with a resounding yes!

Is it easy? Well, maybe it's not easy, but it's definitely *easier* if you have a guide who has "been there, done that" to let you know what works and what doesn't. With Gail's insights and astute understanding, we can identify the undercurrents of power in the workplace and then be able to respond, not just react, when making a powerful choice.

Power Up Power Down is serious (she's a great researcher), humorous (she brings some delightful levity to looking at the ways people disrupt work), and inspirational as Gail shares her own hard-won life lessons about power at work—in the Boardroom and in the Break Room.

Gail's difficult lessons led her to develop real-world tactics and strategies to harness her own power. Now she's giving us the opportunity to understand our power and show us how to use it—ethically and effectively—to make a positive difference for ourselves and the people we work with.

If you've ever felt uncomfortable with the power dynamic at work and haven't been able to "move the needle," *Power Up Power Down* will give you the exact tools you need to become your healthiest, most "power-full" self.

Karen Anderson, MS, Strategic Book Coach, *Wall Street Journal* and *USA Today* Best Selling Author

NOTE FROM THE AUTHOR

Power (and the use and abuse of power) is a hot topic these days, and people are thinking and talking more about power now than perhaps in any other time in history—which is a good thing!

But power is a massive subject. I have written *Power Up Power Down* to focus on power as it plays out in typical workplace situations (even if we're working from home). The stories you will read in *Power Up Power Down* are all true but are an amalgamation of people and situations I've encountered over my career.

That said, we all know there are abuses of power in the workplace. *Power Up Power Down* is not intended to address the range of dynamics that revolve around the misuse of power as it relates to sexual harassment, workplace affairs, inappropriate conduct, and the like.

I am not a counselor, therapist, or lawyer so it is not my intent to give advice for those situations. *So please, if you find yourself in a difficult situation at work or at home, use the resources I provide at the end of the book and get help.* There are skilled and caring people who are available if you need it.

My goal, and the mission of this book, is to spark learning, personal growth, and a deeper understanding of our power in everyday life in the workplace. I want to help us all make the shift to embrace our personal empowerment and become agents of influence and change.

With that said, I invite you to explore with me what power is, how it works, the ways we can use it, and how we can each step into our power positively, effectively, and ethically.

POWER
IS

POWER
UP
POWER
DOWN

POWER
IS NOT

AGGRESSIVE
JUDGMENTAL
CONTEMPTUOUS
SMOTHERING
SELF-ENHANCEMENT
CHAOTIC
GUILT
ATTACKING
BRUTE
ATTRIBUTES
EGO
INSTITUTIONAL
NEGLECTING
ABUSIVE
DISAPPROVING
SCHMOOZING
VENGEFUL
TITLE
PRIVILEGE
YELLING
VIOLENCE
SWEARING
YELLING CALLOUS
SCARY
PERMANENT
MONEY
SCREAMING
DIMINISHING CONTROLLING
RESENTFUL
GUILT CONFLICT
INVASIVE HATEFUL
SUFFOCATING
BACKWARD
MARTYR
NARCISSISTIC PREOCCUPIED LOSE DESTRUCTIVE
BATTLES
VICTIM
POSSESSIONS ABSOLUTE
ABSOLUTE
CHAOTIC
MONEY
GUILT
PHYSICAL
DISTRACTED
HOSTILITY
SELF-RIGHTEOUS
FEELINGS
STATUS
VIOLENT
ANGER PHYSICAL
SCARY
LOSE
SEXUAL
FEAR WIN
CONTEST
ANGER
CRUEL
NARCISSISTIC
CONTROLLING
MONEY
FORCE
STATUS DOMINATING
WIN
ABUSIVE MANIPULATING
CRITICAL MANIPULATING
DEPRESSIVE DOMINATING
SHAMING
ABUSIVE
BIAS
DISAPPROVING CRITICAL HATEFUL
HATEFUL
RESENTFUL
VIOLENT
SENIORITY
EGO STATURE
JUDGMENTAL
DEGRADING
GUILT CENTERED
INTIMIDATION MONEY RESENTFUL
JUDGMENTAL
HARASSING POSITION
YELLING INDIFFERENT
INTOLERANT
SHOWING
PRIVILEGE
SIZE
INSTITUTIONAL
PREOCCUPIED SHAMING
ABANDONING
NEGLECTING
EXCLUDING
EXPLOITATION DIMINISHING
COERCION
PUNISHING
DESTRUCTIVE
INTELLIGENCE
SWEARING
MOVEMENT
PERMANENT
MARTYR CRUEL
VIOLENT
CORRUPTION
POPULARITY
REPRESSION
BULLYING
POWERLESSNESS
RETALIATING
SCARY INVALIDATING
PUNISHMENT
DISAPPROVING
CONTEMPTUOUS
POSSESSIONS FEELINGS
ATTACKING CONFLICT INVASIVE
PHYSICAL
ABSOLUTE

MY POWER JOURNEY

You could say I started out clueless.

Early on in my career, I began to be painfully aware of power and how it is used (and misused) when I began working as the Associate Executive Director at a community foundation. I was the only full-time employee and the other employee was the Executive Director, who worked part-time. He was away from the office more than he was there.

Part of my responsibilities included running the day-to-day operations of the organization, and I always strove to be diligent and hardworking. But more often than not, I did extra work while my boss received extra credit. Knowing I had advanced the foundation beyond what was anticipated and having exceeded the established organizational goals, I decided to ask my boss for a raise.

I went into his office, pulled up a chair, and calmly and professionally ask for an increase in my salary.

His reply, "You don't need a raise. You get child support for the kids, don't you?"

I was stunned. But I quickly responded, "Yes, but that has nothing to do with the job I am doing for the foundation." He rolled his eyes and walked away.

But at the next board meeting, I was encouraged when I saw "salary discussion" on the agenda. The board did approve a salary increase—but it was for *his* salary, not mine.

Given my commitment and efforts, I felt demoralized.

My work and my contributions to the foundation were unnoticed and, I felt, unappreciated. Yet whenever I approached the Executive Director about a raise, he would repeatedly say, "You get child support. You don't need a raise."

Finally, I reached the end of my rope.

Although it was a job I loved, I submitted my resignation and took a position elsewhere. I knew I had contributed in multiple ways to making the organization successful, and I wasn't surprised to learn that the Board of Directors hired three people to fill my position.

What did surprise me was when I realized I had unknowingly given my power away!

As a young, ambitious woman in the workplace, I wasn't always aware of power dynamics, and I didn't always use power properly. Power wasn't something I thought I had at my disposal, especially early on. Looking back, I now know I made many mistakes trying to navigate my role with power and figure out where I fell on the power continuum. And so, I began my power journey to become aware of, and begin to understand, power.

Found It, Then Lost It

What I experienced in that job early in my career was just the tip of the iceberg when it came to my thinking about power. Despite my knowledge, education, and achievements, my voice was too often overlooked or completely ignored. I continued to be successful and serve in high-level leadership positions, but I knew deep down that there was some potential I wasn't achieving.

I often felt like I had handed my power over to someone else instead of having my opinion be heard or considered. I spent almost all of my corporate career in the room... but more often than not, I felt invisible.

I didn't know what the problem was or how to fix it.

A number of years later, I was asked to be the volunteer chair of an International Leadership Summit. I'd been an active member of the host organization for years, so it was quite an honor to chair the event. I was given a budget and, to my excitement, carte blanche to design and create the event.

In that role, I was able to fully use my skills and talents, including negotiating and securing great speakers at reduced rates. The event was much more successful than previous years, both financially and from the reviews of the participants. I received kudos nationally for the Summit's success and finally felt that my accomplishments had been acknowledged and appreciated.

The following year I was asked once again to lead the International Leadership Summit and I anticipated I'd have the same level of success, so I gladly accepted.

But a change in the organization's leadership that year created a perfect storm.

The new leadership had very different ideas on how the Summit should be run. It didn't take long for me to realize that the creative license I was granted before wasn't going to be possible.

This time around, I wasn't allowed to set the agenda or negotiate with speakers. Instead, the organization's leadership stepped around me and contracted with only one speaker, which consumed the majority of the budget. I was left with very limited resources and felt like my hands were tied behind my back—in essence, I was simply a figurehead.

The new leadership was coasting on my name and the successful reputation from the previous year's Summit to draw attendees. I could tell early on that the event wasn't going to be nearly as outstanding as it had been. Despite numerous attempts to share my ideas and express my concerns, I was always dismissed. And to my dismay, my name was still attached.

Self-doubt set in and questions started firing off in my head, "Why didn't they trust me? Hadn't I proved myself last year? Why was I given a title with no power or control?"

As I had feared, the event was nothing like the success it had been the year before. I felt like both my name and reputation got tarnished in the process. Needless to say, my self-confidence plummeted.

Precisely because of these types of situations (some outside my control and others of my own doing), I embarked on a quest to discover what power was and how to use it effectively.

After years of personal and professional blunders, growth, research, and training, I have uncovered some of the main ways power plays out in all of our interactions with other people, but especially in the workplace. Proper use of power can advance and strengthen relationships and help you get a seat at the table and be heard. And the great news is I discovered that power isn't something you either have or don't have—it can be *learned*.

So, *Power Up Power Down* is the culmination of my journey. It is my way of "paying it forward" by offering my experience and what I've learned to others—and help you step into the power that is rightfully yours!

The North Wind and the Sun

The North Wind and the Sun had a quarrel about which of them was the stronger. While they were disputing with much heat and bluster, a Traveler passed along the road wrapped in a cloak.

"Let us agree," said the Sun, "that he is the stronger who can strip that Traveler of his cloak."

"Very well," growled the North Wind and at once sent a cold, howling blast against the Traveler.

With the first gust of wind, the ends of the cloak whipped about the Traveler's body. But he immediately wrapped it closely around him, and the harder the Wind blew, the tighter he held it to him. The North Wind tore angrily at the cloak, but all his efforts were in vain.

Then the Sun began to shine. At first his beams were gentle, and in the pleasant warmth after the bitter cold of the North Wind, the Traveler unfastened his cloak and let it hang loosely from his shoulders. The Sun's rays grew warmer and warmer. The man took off his cap and mopped his brow.

At last the Traveler became so heated that he pulled off his cloak, and to escape the blazing sunshine, threw himself down in the welcome shade of a tree by the roadside.

"Gentleness and kind persuasion win
where force and bluster fail."

CHAPTER ONE

What Is Power?

From the time I was a small child, I was aware of personal power. I think most of us are aware at some level how power plays out from the time we are little.

I was the youngest of four children and my oldest brother was eighteen years my senior. With that kind of age difference, I never felt my voice mattered, and no matter how hard I tried, I was just a pesky five-year-old.

But I wasn't about to give up easily. I definitely found a way to be heard; I yelled at the top of my lungs! Basically, I would "throw a tantrum" and the louder I got, the more my family paid attention.

While this tactic of throwing a tantrum worked when I was young, needless to say, yelling becomes less and less effective as we age. The one power move that I believed served me well when I was little to get some attention (getting louder) actually detracted from me being taken seriously the older I got. However, those same feelings of not being heard persisted for many years.

Growing up, my champion was my dad and when he suddenly died when I was sixteen, the power dynamics in our family changed dramatically. Hoping to find answers through education (my dad had been the school superintendent), I majored in psychology and did some graduate work in behavioral therapy. I even went on to get a master's degree in Human Services Administration, but something was still missing. I still didn't feel very powerful.

After I finished grad school, I worked in the non-profit world for a number of years and had a successful career doing development, consulting, and training.

One crisp, fall morning, I arrived early to attend an executive board meeting for a foundation where I was serving as a consultant. They had asked me to sit in and offer insights and suggestions on how to use the meeting to better engage the board.

During the allotted networking time before this 7 a.m. meeting, a new female board member and I were talking with one of the longtime board members. He was sharing how he had rented a retreat facility to host twenty people, affording them time together to draw on their collective expertise and improve their leadership skills and influence. It sounded interesting, and I was intrigued. I mentioned to him that if he ever had an open spot, I would be very interested in attending.

He replied, "Oh, I'm sorry, it's only for men. I believe men are the true leaders."

Before I could respond, we were interrupted, and he was pulled away. I turned to the woman standing beside me and asked if she had heard and interpreted the statement in the same way I had. She nodded sharply and her lips were pursed. I could see that she was stewing internally, and it wasn't long before she expressed her outrage by stating how she couldn't believe that way of thinking even still existed in this day and age!

Although she remained very poised during the meeting, I could tell she was simmering under the surface as each minute passed. To top it off, this same longtime board member had no qualms about repeating his "only men are invited" statement as he told the rest of the board about the upcoming leadership weekend.

Since I had heard this statement earlier, I was able to observe how the other powerful and prominent female board members reacted to his statement of female exclusion. I could not only sense their distaste, but the same disapproval was reflected among a number of male board members as well.

But guess what? *Nobody challenged him.*

When I looked around the table and realized that no one was going to say anything, I had an epiphany. I finally recognized that nobody takes our power. *We give it away, often with our silence.* In this case, it was through each board member remaining silent about their colleague's egregious statement.

Everyone in that room had willingly (albeit unconsciously) handed over their power in order to keep the peace. Armed with this enlightened understanding, I saw clearly that the future well-being of the foundation's leadership teetered on a precipice.

As the meeting continued, I watched firsthand how the power dynamics changed based on this one man's statement. It was obvious this particular board member had all the power and influence in the meeting while the others were scrambling to reclaim their positioning by kowtowing to him.

As I watched this play out from the sidelines, I saw the verbal and nonverbal interaction of the group shift. And I have to admit, I was in a quandary about what to do.

As the consultant, it wasn't my place to call him out, especially not publicly.

My solution was simple but actually quite strategic. When I got the opportunity, I addressed the board as a whole and asked the question: "With the weekend coming up that's only open to a limited number of people, what other opportunities are available for other members of the leadership team?"

One of the female board members let the group know of a high-end leadership workshop being offered that was still open. And in fact, she offered to sponsor anyone who wanted to attend.

As I continued to watch this scenario play out, it dawned on me. Changing the power balance in the room can happen with the right understanding of how power dynamics work.

It wasn't just about men vs. women or older vs. younger. There was something else at play.

It was then I decided that somehow, someway, I would find a way to level the playing field.

Power Defined

Let's start by making sure we're on the same page with the definition of power. There are lots of perceptions about what power is.

In some ways, describing power is like describing the wind. You know it's there and you can feel it, but it's hard to put into words.

Throughout time, power has taken on many meanings, but the power we are talking about is not as simple as putting gas in a car and stepping on the accelerator to propel the vehicle forward.

The power I'm talking about is that unseen mysterious energy that exists between each of us and how its use can either increase or decrease our ability to influence and accomplish our goals. Harnessing this power the right way leads to positive interactions with others, getting things done, and creates an environment where cooperation and diversity can flourish.

At its most basic level, power can be channeled by aligning our mindset, body movements, and verbal inflection. Much like plugging a lamp into an outlet, we need to plug into the appropriate power response in any given situation.

This interpersonal energy is central to every one of our interactions. Yes, every interaction. Power is an inherent social contract. When you are dealing with family, friends, coworkers, or strangers, there is always an element of power in play.

This unseen power element isn't male or female, white or black, boss or employee, or any other contrasting element. It is gender, race, and hierarchically neutral. Power is defined simply as "the capacity or ability to direct or influence the behavior of others or the course of events." It's an energy that ebbs and flows as we interact with others.

Power just exists.

That said, there's often a "look" to those who appear powerful to us, and we subconsciously perceive it. It's communicated in the way people stand, take up space, and use their vocal tonality. In fact, our brain gives twelve times more significance to gestures and body language than words.

How we communicate nonverbally (energetically) plays a huge role in our ability to express our power.

Power and Energy

The idea of energy around power hit home for me when I was at an event and a surprise celebrity came into the room.

In my role as a corporate fundraiser, I've had the opportunity to meet many exceptional people who were generous in their philanthropy.

One evening, I was invited to a small dinner party given by one of our very committed donors at his country club. He told me he had invited an out-of-town friend to join us and there would be just seven of us for dinner.

I was mingling with him and a few of the other guests when he saw his friend come to the door. He turned to the group and said, "Hey, everyone, I'd love for you to meet my dear friend, Morgan Freeman."

As you can imagine, having an Academy Award-winning actor walk in changed the atmosphere in the room!

Known for his diverse roles in movies such as *Driving Miss Daisy*, *Shawshank Redemption*, and the comedy *Bruce Almighty* (where he played God), Morgan Freeman is a formidable force.

Sitting at the table that night, he exuded power, not because of anything he said, but just by his presence alone. You could feel the shift in the room as this accomplished actor arrived to have a normal dinner with friends. His energy was powerful.

But is this kind of energy and power just reserved for celebrities? Not in the least.

People who understand how to harness their innate interpersonal power give off cues and signals that are indicators of power and influence, even if they're not obvious.

Sadly, too many people can feel powerless even when they actually aren't (often this is rooted in limiting self-beliefs). I believe there is always personal power to be accessed, and it is up to each of us to step into our power responsibly and with integrity—because choice leads to power.

What I mean by this is when we choose how and when to manage our power, we ultimately take control. We make better decisions than when we react in a knee-jerk way.

In fact, people who understand (and practice) how to access their power in intentional and ethical ways become more self-assured and have more confidence in their thoughts and ideas. Power and self-assurance are cyclical: The more confident a person, the more power they believe they deserve.

There's no need to seek permission from others on whether we are worthy of having power or influence; *we already have it.* Whether we realize it or not, each one of us has power and influence. It is an ever-present dynamic in all interactions. Power is not just relegated to those in exclusive "circles;" we can all consciously choose to use it appropriately.

And the best news... tapping into our power allows us to use mistakes, failures, and setbacks as guideposts for growth and learning.

Real power works by energizing us from a place of stability and self-worth, not by demanding control.

That's why it is essential to reflect on our personal understanding and relationship with power.

The Road from Frustration to Empowerment

As I continued to think about and study how power works, I enrolled in the Entrepreneurial Leadership Certification program from the Graduate School of Business at Stanford University.

Stanford provided me with great insight into business fundamentals, human behavior, and negotiation with others. They also showed me how each of these skills could be taught and learned.

One of the courses I took was specifically about power and its impact in the workplace.

To demonstrate how we perceive the power continuum, the professor passed around a playing card to each student. The "value" of each card represented a position within a company. The Aces, Kings, and Queens were the C-suite executives, the Jacks, 10s, and 9s were middle management, and the 8s through 1s were employees.

Without looking at our card, we held it so others could see its value. Everyone began milling around the room, interacting with others based on their "position" within the company. If you came across someone in possession of a King, you were supposed to treat them as you would a CEO or other high-level leader. When speaking to a person with a numeric card, you were to interact with them in a manner that someone in this position would expect.

At the end of this exercise, we self-selected our place in the company based on how our interactions with others played out: Leadership, Middle Management, or Lower-Level Employee.

Every person in the room chose the correct category in the company.

Why? Because conversations with and treatment from others showed us where we fell on the power continuum.

Doing this exercise helped me to see how our words and perceptions impacted how we interacted with others. (And I have to say, I was a tiny bit embarrassed to realize how easy it was to type people.)

Soon after, in one of my Business Negotiation classes, the professor assigned an interactive exercise during which we were each teamed up with another student. At the time, I had no idea how this seemingly simple exercise would impact my thinking so profoundly for years to come.

The professor gave each participant a goal to achieve; we had to negotiate with our partner and work toward obtaining our desired result. Neither party knew the other's goal. If we reached an impasse, we could forfeit and still receive credit for the assignment. But the desired outcome was to reach the goal we had been assigned.

My partner came out like she had on boxing gloves and was almost combative in trying to achieve her goal. She would not acquiesce in any way and was adamant about what she wanted. She absolutely refused to budge. I was exasperated. We went around in circles, made absolutely no progress, and ending up forfeiting.

We were all shocked when we learned in the debrief that every one of us had been assigned the same goal; *it was the process of getting there* that the professor wanted us to learn.

Teams received points by reaching a negotiation that benefited *both* parties. Some teams negotiated but had points taken away because no mutually beneficial outcome was reached. Those teams approached the negotiation as a "win/*lose*" situation.

The negotiation role-play has stuck with me ever since and eventually changed the focus of my career. Power is *not* about win/lose. It is creating a win/win and arriving at mutually beneficial outcomes for all involved—no matter who they are or what power dynamic is going on.

This revelation struck me to my core, and I knew I was on the right track.

Authentic Leadership

While I was working as a consultant and studying the impact of power at Stanford, my frustrations with how power was being played out in the workplace were leading me, vocationally, in a new direction. But I wasn't sure what direction to take.

I met my good friend, Sarah, for lunch one day and had a heart-to-heart conversation with her. She recognized (and pointed out to me) that I actually had a lot of entrepreneurial spirit in me and suggested I check out John Maxwell.

(If you're not familiar with John Maxwell, he's been an internationally respected leadership expert, speaker, trainer, coach, and author for more than forty years. His philosophy is simple: "*Everything rises and falls on leadership.*" He's a #1 *New York Times* best-selling author of over seventy-seven books, with more than twenty-four million volumes sold in fifty languages.)

When Sarah suggested I take the Maxwell leadership training to become a certified coach, speaker, and trainer, something in my gut told me this was exactly where I needed to be.

It was during this time that I began to more clearly identify the importance of power and influence. One of John's famous quotes is, "*Leadership is influence: nothing more, nothing less.*"

I had my "aha" moment when I realized my self-image and beliefs were creating barriers that often stood in the way of me reaching my highest potential. Through the Maxwell training, I learned that we all have our own belief systems, which unconsciously impact us unless we choose to bring them to the surface and address them head-on.

After a lot of soul searching and self-reflection, I identified my own belief systems. This gave me a much-needed look into how I was standing in my own way when stepping into my use of power and influence.

I recognized how my lack of boundaries, misconstrued values, and poor self-image had caused me, and so many others, to forfeit power and control.

It quickly became apparent that I was not the only person who struggled with having a voice, maintaining control, and creating win/win situations.

Everywhere I looked, the same issues of power and influence were bubbling to the surface. I was intrigued and began to document and research what I observed. There were approaches that always worked, approaches that appeared to work only for some people, and some approaches that never worked.

I was on a quest to find out more, and in the following pages, I'll share some of what I discovered with you.

CHAPTER TWO

Power and Choice

n the northeastern United States, cod fishing is a big commercial business. There is a market for eastern cod all over the United States, especially in sections farthest removed from the northeast coastline.

But the demand for cod posed a problem. Sometimes it had to be shipped thousands of miles away while still maintaining freshness and flavor. Initially, the cod was frozen prior to shipping, but freezing this fish took away almost all of the flavor. Bewildered, shippers experimented by sending the cod alive in tanks of seawater, but that proved even worse. Not only was it more expensive to ship in this manner, but the cod still lost their flavor, and in addition, became soft and mushy en route.

Then a very creative person solved the problem in a most curious way. The cod were placed in a tank of water along with their natural predator, which in this case is the catfish. These two fish are natural enemies in the wild.

From the time the cod left the East Coast until they arrived at their westernmost destination, those ornery catfish chased the cod all over the tank. The most amazing thing happened. When the cod arrived at the market, they were as fresh as the day they were first caught. There was no loss of flavor nor was the texture affected. If anything, they tasted *better*. They actually were strengthened because of the adversity.

Who ended up being more powerful—the catfish or the cod? (I know they both get eaten but just go with me here.)

It's not too far-fetched for us to think of ourselves as residing in an environment or "tank" where we need to learn and grow to create the best version of ourselves. This process happens to each of us in our own way.

Yes, it can be painful and sometimes almost unbearable to be in a place of adversity. But it is precisely this process that keeps us from becoming stagnant in our quest to grow and increases our potential. Like the cod, we need difficult situations in our lives to keep us sharp, actively grow, and strengthen our character.

Even though we may feel at times as if we are being eaten by power predators in our lives, we are stronger and smarter than each of us realizes.

Our Struggle with Power

I've often been asked why it is that we struggle with power in so many places in our lives. I wish I had a definitive answer, but although it's not *the* answer, I do have some ideas that may shed some light, and here's where some great news comes in.

We have a conscious choice to make; we can look at other people and situations as our natural enemy where our fear of power comes into play. Or we can flip the script and realize these people and situations are here to help us grow and strengthen our ability and character.

Entering power with the correct attitude gives us the capability to overcome challenging circumstances in our lives. Whether we like it or not, each and every one of us has these "fish" in our lives and are presented with choices on how to handle them.

Our Language Around Power

Let's start by looking at how we talk and think about power. Power, both verbal and nonverbal, is a communication—it's language!

We easily recognize the language of power in all of our interactions, and we intuitively understand our place on the power continuum in any given circumstance.

But first, we'll look at the negative expression of power. Power is *not* about dominance, coercion, or hostility. It is not part of a contest, it is not owned, and it is most definitely not permanent. Power is not about defining our personal worth or cloaking our insecurities.

But power is happening no matter what, consciously or unconsciously. We can claim our power or we can relinquish it—the choice is ours.

When used properly, power is a resource we can use to create a win/win situation and impact our ability to effect positive change—even if it's only within ourselves.

Power should *not* be viewed as a battle in which we win and someone else loses.

When we use our power and influence *properly*, we maintain relationships, grow ourselves, and we become more accepting of other people and their ideas. This reclaiming of our power in any situation is what creates a win/win.

Adopting this mindset allows us to walk an empowered path, lift others, set and respect boundaries, and positively reframe what we believe about ourselves and those around us.

In fact, using power consciously and purposefully allows us to raise our awareness and learn how to respond. We become strategic stewards of our life, emotions, attitudes, and behaviors.

Whether we are in a face-to-face meeting, on a video conference, or at a concert with 5,000 people, one thing remains consistent: Power is at play in every situation.

So, What Exactly Does Power Up Power Down Mean?

When talking about power, it might be easy to assume that all power should be equal. But the power balances we are talking about are more about handling power differences the right way to make the most of the potential influence in every situation. Power is that energy that flows in every interaction, which creates a positive or negative experience.

What I've discovered is there is a law and process when it comes to power. The law is *we only have the ability to change ourselves; we have no control over others.* Now it may seem like that's a "no-brainer" that we all know to be true. But in the context of power, by changing ourselves, we can change the way people view us, interact with us, and as a result, change the experience.

Power Up Power Down is the *ability to remain in control of ourselves in any situation to make an intentional choice in how we respond in the moment.*

One of the most profound quotes I've ever heard comes from Viktor Frankl, an Austrian neurologist, psychiatrist, and Holocaust survivor. He said, "Between stimulus and response there is a space. In that space is our power to choose our response. In our response lies our growth and our freedom."

True personal power is the intentional use of the space between any given stimulus and our response.

The law of power expresses itself through our mindset, beliefs, and boundaries. That's why it's crucial to know what's going on internally because it's the foundation for what happens externally.

Reacting in the moment and losing our temper or emotions in any situation only gives our power away.

When we have self-respect, self-love, self-worth, and self-confidence, our stage is solid, firm, and ready to withstand the elements. Everything else that happens externally—roles, situations, and people—changes continually. When our foundation is a solid platform, we are better equipped to respond appropriately, step into the proper power role, change to a new script, and/or create something new.

Having the presence of mind to recognize what's going on in the moment and respond with intentionality is the catalyst for self-control and becoming empowered.

Making the Choice to Power Up or Power Down

Remember, power leads to choice, and choice leads to power. So, here's a simple way I like to think of Powering Up or Powering Down.

Powering Up or Powering Down is both about how you control yourself and also how you present yourself.

Powering Up is the choice you make to step into a fuller presence.

Powering Down is the choice you make to change your stance to retract as an intentional response.

For example, think of a male peacock. These colorful creatures boast impressively sized and patterned plumage that they fan out for display purposes.

Powering Up is like displaying their showy plumage, big and impressive.

Powering Down is like when they fold their feathers into their train. They are still the same bird, and the feathers are all there, it's just a matter of what's showing.

We often don't think about whether to Power Up or Power Down. We think our reaction just happens. But what we are discovering is that real personal power is being able to make that choice to go full feathers or folded train.

The true power is in the choice.

Learning to Respond, Not React

Power Up Power Down is all about moving out of a reactive, habitual state into a state of consciousness where we can be creative and purposeful.

By changing things about ourselves and how we interact, we can properly step into our power, creating a significant impact with those around us.

In a way, power is a role. We learn to play our part and use the influence that is available to us. There is a language that goes with power. It begins internally with our thoughts, then filters externally into our movements and behavior.

In my experience as a consultant, I have found myself in some very interesting spots, and when I was working with one particular small company, the power of *responding not reacting* became evident.

There were three of us at the boardroom table: the president, the vice president (both men), and me as the consultant. The vice president, Jake, was what some might refer to as a "brown-noser." He never challenged the president, even if he knew the president's idea wouldn't be accepted (or worse, never implemented) by the team.

I had attended enough meetings to see that Jake often manipulated the president through his constant praise and agreement but would sabotage ideas that came from other members of the team. In fact, he often would get ideas from other team members and use them as his own. He would not communicate with his colleagues, and the other members of the team would be left in the dust as Jake stalled them and pressed forward himself. He was very reluctant to share any type of successes with other team members. Although the president was basically a good guy and a force to be reckoned with, he was pulled in multiple directions, and his focus was the bottom line—he was never able to pay attention to how company advancement happened.

As a seasoned female executive, I knew that trying to push my way between these two high-ego men could negatively affect me. So, I chose to move the company's agenda forward, knowing that even though both of them needed some personal behavior changes, it was not my job to address that with them. I only had the ability to change my approach and, hopefully, change the outcomes. I decided to focus them by coming from a "question approach."

From that day forward, I showed up in Power Up mode. At meetings, I expanded my space over two seats, and I began to intentionally use words that communicated competence, such as "productive," "effective," "efficient," and "streamline." I made sure my tone of voice was always slow and low.

I pushed myself to insert pauses and get comfortable with silence. I began asking questions like,

- "What is the goal of this project?"
- "Did anyone else talk about doing something like this?"
- "What is the best way to collaborate with other team members?"
- "Who on the team can we get that has knowledge about this?"

And then I said, "As leaders, let's set the task force to bring this project to fruition."

I always begin with the assumption that people are doing the best they can at the moment. It was not my job to change Jake. And by focusing on the task at hand and not Jake's behavior (as inappropriate as it may have been), I was able to lead him into collaboration with his coworkers and increase the productivity of the team… and sidestep a power struggle.

In this case, there was a need for me to Power Up. Other times, I've been in situations where there was a need to Power Down.

By holding onto the knowledge that we are all equally valuable and deserve respect, recognition, and appreciation, we can fully harness our power and make the best choices.

The "secret sauce" is using intuition, self-talk, and boundaries to help us step into our power.

Our Amazing Automatic Brain

I'll tell you more about this a bit later, but let's start by looking at our extraordinary brain and how it works.

When talking about being able to make choices, it's natural for, "Well, I just can't help it" to come up. We humans possess two very unique ways of assessing and analyzing information. In short, we have basically two ways of processing and coming to decisions and actions—our fast-thinking brain and slow-thinking brain.

The fast-thinking brain, also referred to as System 1 in *Thinking, Fast and Slow* by Nobel laureate Daniel Kahneman, is a decision-making center that forms quick judgments and decisions based on emotion and impressions.

A fast-thinking brain is spontaneous, immediate, and non-deliberate. Processing in our fast-thinking brain is automatic, frequent, emotional, stereotypical, and most importantly, unconscious. It bypasses our slow-thinking, rational brain, and we arrive at conclusions we're not even consciously aware of.

This fast-thinking process serves us well in many cases. Information is taken in and processed rapidly, often keeping us out of harm's way and freeing up our logical mind to make conscious, thoughtful conclusions.

Always active and on alert, the fast-thinking processor makes us swerve to safety when a car suddenly moves into our lane on the highway. It makes us scream when a spider crawls on us; it tells us when an object is too hot to touch. It enables us to read large text on billboards, solve 2 + 2, and gauge the general distance between objects.

If we had to reason and rationalize all of this information, not only would our physical safety be in jeopardy, but we would be mentally exhausted and unable to focus on tasks that required our diligent attention.

This immediate ability to react quickly served our hunter-gatherer ancestors incredibly well. Still, as humans have developed, our instantaneous brain continues to make snap judgments that are often outside our awareness and control. When we become skilled at a task, like driving or riding a bike, it becomes second nature. This results in that function no longer requiring an excessive amount of deliberate mental effort, and the skill is filed away in the fast-thinking brain.

Our fast-thinking brain forms many of the decisions we make every day. We unconsciously accept the good majority of those judgments without further analysis. To overcome our inherent biases and limiting self-beliefs, we must become more aware of when we should trust this process versus when we need to slow down and logically analyze our decisions and beliefs. This is where the "I just can't help it" comment comes into play.

Our slow-thinking brain allows us time to consciously reason through an issue and discern facts and truths before judgment. This time-consuming process involves considerable mental effort and, as such, is left for analyzing problems our fast-thinking brain can't quickly and efficiently resolve. Our slow-thinking, rational mind is reserved for calculation and analysis, comprehending complicated content, and logical and effortful problem-solving processes.

So, the slow-thinking brain plays out this way in our everyday lives; we are continually taking in information, arriving at judgments, decisions, feelings, and impressions around what we have experienced. After we have encountered enough of these similar impressions or had a significant emotional event around an experience to ingrain it deeply, it becomes endorsed by our fast-thinking brain and becomes an automatic response or habit.

In California's Central Valley, the winter months are cold and damp thanks to the heavy, low-lying tule fog that forms after the first significant rainfall. This wet blanket can block the sky and cause hazardous driving conditions for days on end.

Orchards and fields are prevalent in this agricultural center of California. Traveling to one of the nearby towns or cities often entails driving two-lane rural roads, with many cross streets but very few traffic lights. This impenetrable, oppressively gray fog cloaks items until they are mere feet away—often too late to react.

In tule fog, a very conscious slow-thinking brain takes the wheel. These conditions don't lend themselves to the spontaneous reactions of the fast-thinking, autopilot brain. Instead, intense focus is required. It is critical to drive well below the speed limit to provide ample time to react. It is also imperative to stop at every intersection and roll down the windows to listen for oncoming cars before proceeding.

Just think if all driving entailed this incredible level of concentration! We would be so mentally exhausted by the time we arrived at our destination that it would be near-impossible to focus on work, school, or whatever else lay at the end of that journey.

To allow ourselves to have a heightened awareness around our unconscious beliefs, thoughts, feelings, and impressions, we need to purposefully downshift. Taking time to rationalize and analyze information can often shed a bright light on what is really a snap judgment or belief we've accepted as true without ample evidence.

In keeping with the driving analogy, we have all been cut off in traffic. I don't know about you, but I've frequently caught myself thinking, "Wow, that person is rude, obnoxious, and thinks where they have to go is more important than the rest of us." Our fast brain creates a story about this person based on very little evidence and accepts it as true. The next time someone cuts us off, the story replays and reinforces that belief as true.

Catching ourselves in these autopilot thoughts and beliefs is powerful. These are the snap judgments and assumptions we leap to, thanks to our fast brain being so, well… fast.

But let's consider that, all too often, we don't have all of the facts to really make that assessment. Maybe the person honestly didn't see us. Maybe they had to move out of the way because something was in their path of travel. Maybe they just spilled scalding hot coffee on themselves. We don't know.

Daniel Kahneman says that one of the most reliable ways to make people believe in falsehoods is frequent repetition. Familiarity, he says, is not something our brain can easily distinguish from truth. It doesn't matter where this misinformation comes from. As long as it is repeated again and again, our fast brain accepts it as true.

Thoughts about ourselves are also managed by our fast-thinking brain. That's why making a commitment to notice them and downshift is so powerful. Ask yourself: Are these ideas and beliefs grounded in fact, or are they formed by years of repetitive and defeating self-talk?

CHAPTER THREE

Power of Mindset

n 2019, I had the privilege of traveling with John Maxwell to Asunción, the capital and largest city in Paraguay, South America. Our mission was to provide assistance to the residents as they began to rebuild and transform the nation from oppression. It was an eye-opening experience.

When I visited a local junior high school, I was distressed to learn that most of the students lived in flimsy cardboard houses that lined the street to the school. When at school, children took their chairs from one classroom to the next just to have a place to sit.

The school building itself was beyond basic. The floors were packed dirt. Thick metal bars lined the windows, which had no panes of glass. In a grave voice, the principal told me that most students were hungry and malnourished, and it was obvious that hygiene was also a huge issue.

He shared the devastating news that most of the students had lost their homes just a couple of weeks before when a fierce storm had unleashed extreme amounts of rain, literally washing away their already fragile houses.

The principal spoke of how the local lumber store donated wood to build new homes for those families whose houses were lost. Many children missed school because it was far more important for them to build a new home for their family. The new houses weren't any more substantial than the last ones, with cardboard walls adhered to the newly constructed wooden framework.

If their homes were unstable, their futures weren't much better. The principal explained that most of the girls would be pregnant by the time they reached high school, and a good majority of the boys would live a life of crime.

It was a cruel circle of life. Depending on their gender, each child's future had seemingly one path: becoming an unwed teen mother or being incarcerated.

But I had hope. The program I was there to share with the teachers and students was about decision-making. The school had implemented a similar curriculum a few years earlier, and the principal was optimistic, saying that they were starting to see progress. The junior high faculty had begun to notice a slight shift in the students choosing a different path, making better decisions than those they believed destiny had laid out for them. Some were choosing to go on to high school.

My whole purpose for being at the school was to help these young students see that today's decisions are what determine their future. As I started to work with these teens, I quickly realized that their view of themselves (their belief system) was their primary obstacle. Knowing I had to find a way to break through their innate bias about themselves, I shared a story with them.

The evening before, I met a group of young musicians who called themselves the "Junkyard Orchestra." This group of Paraguayan children was no different than the students sitting in front of me. They, too, were incredibly poor. They also slept in cardboard houses and struggled every day to find a decent meal. However, the children in the orchestra had changed their thinking from, "There is no way" to "Let's find a way."

In Paraguay, a violin costs as much as a house. So, even if a family could somehow find the money to buy such an instrument for their child, it would make their son or daughter a target for thieves and violence. But these kids were determined to find a way to make music. Embracing their "Let's find a way" mindset, they went to the junkyard, gathered discarded objects, and crafted their instruments out of what most of us would consider garbage.

Discarded metal pizza pans were transformed into violins, and petroleum drums became cellos. Turning over his instrument, a ten-year-old boy showed me the burn marks on his "violin." Triangle caution icons decorated the front of these junkyard "cellos." These kids had literally hammered and bent scraps of garbage to create instruments that, believe it or not, played beautiful music.

As I sat listening to them play, I closed my eyes. I may not be a music aficionado, but I couldn't tell the difference between the "homemade" violins and cellos these young musicians played and the expensive ones crafted from beautiful wood.

There was nothing different about the opportunities these Paraguayan children had over the students I was teaching. They didn't have more resources, better homes, more food, or increased access to things.

When we embrace the "there is no way" mentality, it perpetuates our feelings and beliefs of inadequacy, both internally and externally.

Fortunately, we have a choice about how we approach power. If we're not aware, our belief system can unconsciously manipulate us, hijacking our ability to respond thoughtfully and see the opportunities that present themselves.

When we have the right mindset, it opens unlimited opportunities and creativity.

For these Junkyard Orchestra kids, their mindset and "Let's find a way" attitude created something beautiful out of garbage and changed the trajectory of their lives.

> *"If you realized how powerful your thoughts are, you would never think a negative thought."*
>
> **– Peace Pilgrim**

Fixed and Growth Mindsets

Before we can talk about regaining power, it's essential to look at how mindset plays a role in our belief systems. Mindset plays a hugely influential role in who we are and how we respond to people, situations, and experiences. Our mindset, like with the children in Paraguay, is a choice and directly tied to our power.

That's why it's important to identify our mindset and look at how it ties into our conscious and unconscious belief system.

Essentially, there are only two kinds of mindsets: fixed and growth.

If a person adopts a fixed mindset, they believe skills are something we're born with; they're set and remain unchangeable. They believe new skills can't be learned and existing skills can't be improved upon. These individuals avoid challenges and constructive feedback triggers them to feel defensive and "take it personally." The fixed mindset person views setbacks as failure, which they attribute as the fault of others.

People with fixed mindsets will often portray themselves as victims. They fail to accept the consequences of their own behavior; instead, they blame others. They often use this victim mentality to gain sympathy, avoid the truth, and dodge the insight that could help them learn and grow. A telltale sign of being in a fixed mindset is someone who tends to "sit on a throne of victimhood."

The opposite is true of a person who adopts a growth mindset. They believe new skills can be achieved through hard work, and they always strive to achieve mastery. As the name implies, these individuals believe challenges should be embraced as opportunities to learn and grow. Their effort is directly related to their success, and they view feedback as critical in identifying areas of improvement. The growth mindset individual believes setbacks are actually a setup for something better in the future—they are signals to prompt new exploration of ways to succeed.

Those possessing a growth mindset have a love of learning, are resilient, implement strategies for improvement, and search for learning opportunities.

Our mindset around life has a direct link to how we view power. Whether it is fixed or focused on growth, it will become the catalyst to move us forward or hold us back. This choice is a personal one. However, if we're to take the reins of power, we must commit ourselves to holding a growth mindset.

Power Begins in Us!

In my work as an executive coach and trainer, I sadly see the impact of self-limiting beliefs all too often. They hamper us in our work and personal lives. And unfortunately, more often than not, those beliefs are self-imposed. Our internal broken record incessantly parrots, "I can't."

A person will only go as far as their thoughts and beliefs about themselves. In order to harness our power correctly, we first must examine what we think and believe about ourselves.

Each of us constructs our belief system over time from influences and experiences that begin when we are young children. A part of our belief system originates from one or more significant life events as well as from those who were influential in our lives.

Throughout our childhood and into adulthood, this belief system is continually reinforced. These ingrained systems can create biases—many of which we possess about ourselves. These oversights about ourselves and others are often unconscious. They have been hardwired into our brains over many years and typically don't surface unless we make a concerted effort to become aware of them.

Choosing to unearth and explore these thoughts, ideas, and beliefs shows us how to overcome and reframe what doesn't serve us well. Bringing our unconscious biases about ourselves (and others) to the forefront enables us to heighten our self-awareness and open ourselves up to relearning new and better ways to believe and deal with hidden habits, including the ability to respond appropriately rather than reacting from a place that isn't in our or anyone's best interest.

Thoughtful and intentional responses impact our power and influence. When we're able to examine ourselves and gain some understanding and insight, we can then effectively manage difficult situations and personalities with calm confidence and certainty, while building lasting and respectful relationships based on trust.

The Power of Self-Reflection

You might have heard it said that we become what we believe about ourselves—and that certainly rings true for me.

Thoughts and beliefs are what propel us to success or contribute to our downfall. Our mindset and beliefs influence how we (consciously or unconsciously) act and behave in ways that move us toward—or away from—success. If we believe in ourselves, we can and will "succeed" no matter what our circumstances. As I said earlier, those who hold a "Let's find a way" outlook behave and act in ways that ensure they ultimately achieve what they believe.

What's the key to our mindset? Being blatantly honest with ourselves.

I know from experience that it's not always easy to dig deep inside ourselves to unearth and reflect on what we believe. But the process allows us to become aware of the self-talk that may be auto-playing in our minds.

I've discovered, and research supports, that to truly succeed and fully step into our power, the first step is to stop the self-defeating, self-condemning thoughts and feelings that tell us we are not "enough."

If we start investigating ourselves deeply with eyes wide open, we'll discover that we are all profoundly intriguing and amazingly fascinating. No one is perfect. We've all made mistakes, but those things alone do not define us. What does define us is our willingness to *compassionately* self-assess and embrace opportunities to grow.

I love the words of author and shame researcher, Brené Brown, *"Only when we are brave enough to explore the darkness will we discover the infinite power of our light."*

It is not an easy task to do the work of changing our thoughts and moving into a better version of ourselves. These self-defeating thoughts are often formed out of fear, focusing on age, past discouragement, guilt, money, education, health, time, weight, self-confidence—the list goes on. We all too quickly accept and internalize these ideas about who we are and what we are worthy of, creating a laundry list of things to tear us down.

But the negative beliefs we have about ourselves will eventually become unhealthy habits that intimidate and hold us back. And over time, they'll get programmed into our subconscious, eroding our self-worth and limiting our ability to properly stand in our power.

Of course, it can be very uncomfortable to sit in the space of self-analysis. When we are honest with ourselves, we naturally conjure up the extreme discomfort of past hurt and pain. By flinging the door open, we are bound to uncover something that makes us cringe (and if you don't, chances are you may not be looking deeply enough!).

But denying that cringe-worthy experience exists doesn't make it disappear. Instead, it adds fuel to the fire of our limiting beliefs with damaging thoughts like, "I don't really have anything to contribute" or "I just don't want to go there."

(Please hear this: I'm not talking about past abuse or trauma. If you have been injured in any way, physically or emotionally, make it a point to get help *now*. Seek out a professional to help work through what has happened and help you become who you are meant to be.)

What I'm addressing here is the process of looking at our limiting beliefs for what they are… things that didn't work or options we tried that we won't try again. Acknowledging these conscious or unconscious beliefs and taking responsibility for them moves us forward into growth and acceptance. This newfound freedom allows us to loosen up and let go of the knots of shame, fear, and guilt that bind us and sap our power.

The Powerful Role of Our Thoughts

Let's consider some of the phrases we may find our subconscious habitually handing out. Much of this self-talk doesn't serve us well, but it continually replays in our minds like a broken record. You may have heard the saying that "we wouldn't talk to a friend the way we talk to ourselves." That's because many of us have such shaming and defeating self-talk.

Negative talk and judgmental conversations in our head sap our energy, self-worth, and power. Our minds tend to get caught in a negative thought loop, and it takes concerted effort to transition to a more optimistic (and powerful) place. There's a difference between obsessively berating ourselves about our flaws and reviewing ourselves to remain honest so we can change and grow. We need to know our strengths and weaknesses and how to leverage them while foregoing self-flagellation.

Personal empowerment requires us to begin to replace these repetitive and self-depleting thoughts with inspiring words that will begin to shift our mindset to a space that is more encouraging, loving, and kind. Below are examples of how to shift negative phrases into self-affirming ones.

- I can't = I can
- I don't believe = I know
- I'm bad at = I will
- I'm afraid = I am confident
- It's impossible = Anything is possible
- I don't have any power = Today is the day I choose to take my power back

What we choose to think and believe can be inspirational catalysts, motivating us to strive, achieve, and succeed. Or they can hold us back, sabotaging and undermining our goals, our self-worth, and our interpersonal power.

The Mind as a Computer

How things are processed in our conscience and unconscious mind is the key to many of our ideas, beliefs, and judgments. (I find the brain fascinating!)

I remember when I first learned to drive a car. I got in, closed the door, and concentrated on my mental checklist: fastening my seat belt, adjusting the mirrors, placing my foot firmly on the brake, and turning the key. All of this was done deliberately and consciously before the car was even running. Each time I went around a curve or made a turn, I went through a step-by-step thought process about when I needed to let off the gas and where in the curve it was safe to accelerate. Every move I made while driving took concerted mental effort.

Now I am able to hop into the car, quickly get situated, and head on my way with ease. Why? Because now that I've been driving for so long, that skill has become automatic, leaving my conscious mind free to think about something else as I am en route to my destination.

When something becomes learned or mastered over time, we no longer have to process and analyze those tasks.

So much of what we experience every day is handled in this manner. These mental assessments are often so fleeting that we aren't aware of them because they never reach conscious awareness.

When we walk down the street and see someone smiling, our brain assesses their expression and decides they are friendly. When we see someone scowling, we make a judgment, often without realizing it, that they are probably angry or annoyed. The information used to make these decisions is extremely limited, but since it fits within the parameters we have experienced before, our brain makes this judgment, and on we go.

This is also true of the voices in our head and our programming. These have become habits that, over time, become entrenched. They seep into our unconscious, lessening our awareness of them and making them all the more difficult to break.

But the key to getting rid of those negative beliefs is *replacing* them. Two thoughts can't occupy the same place so putting a positive thought in will drive the negative thought out!

Dr. Bruce Lipton is a stem cell biologist and a renowned speaker known for bridging science and spirit. His work reveals revolutionary scientific discoveries of how our bodies and minds are genetically intertwined.

I find the analogy he offers very interesting. He proposes the idea that the human brain is like our personal computer. As with all computers, it requires programming to operate. Much of that programming is behind the scenes, telling our lungs to breathe, our heart to pump, and all of our other autonomic responses to function. Dr. Lipton describes this as our "operating system," something built-in and over which we have no control. Humans are hardwired with this systemic functionality from the moment of birth.

Layered on top of a computer's operating system is software created to perform additional tasks. Translating this analogy to our mind as a computer, we also have add-on programming generated by what has been "inputted" into our brain throughout our life. These include experiences we've had, what people tell us about ourselves, what we read, the ideas and beliefs we are exposed to, the company we keep, and of course, our self-talk.

Living in the middle of Silicon Valley, I often hear a popular phase in the tech world referring to computers and programming:

Garbage in, garbage out. If we choose to fuel our brain with toxic, harmful, or self-defeating concepts, we program our mind to regurgitate that same information right back to us.

Changing the way I talk to myself has helped me learn to be unapologetically confident—as each of us can be. Confident doesn't mean cocky, but rather possessing an assuredness that our voice matters and that we matter. We each possess unique gifts, talents, perspectives, and knowledge, and we should take pride in them. Confidence is knowing we can both learn from as well as teach others.

Standing in the awareness and confidence of who we are helps us grow stronger so we can become a better version of ourselves. It is a muscle that needs to be exercised regularly. And just like we wouldn't think about exercising our body only occasionally, daily exercising our mind through positive self-talk is a great place to start intentionally working out our confidence.

"Through Us, Not to Us"

One of the worst examples of garbage programming we can adopt is the belief that we can change others. We spend too much precious time and energy trying to fix other people. This only avoids addressing the real work needed—self-reflection, internal change, and reprogramming our limiting beliefs. Engaging in this ineffective process expends endless amounts of energy over something we can't control. This results in yet another source of giving our power away and is sure to present a relentless battle we are doomed to lose.

It is so much easier to see others' faults and point out what they need to do to fix themselves. It is an age-old problem. Jesus even said, "How can you say to your brother, 'let me take the speck out of your eye,' when there is the log in your own eye?"

I have to admit, I'm guilty of looking outward instead of inward. It is less painful to tell others what to do rather than focusing on leading myself. This outward focus is a distraction. The real issue at hand is eliminating the "garbage" in our personal software.

We only possess the power to change ourselves. We cannot change anything or anyone outside of ourselves, because life is happening *through* us and not *to* us. Once we understand this fundamental truth, we can begin to replace self-judgment with self-fascination. This process enables us to turn a massive corner on embracing and harnessing our internal power.

Unfortunately, there are people in our lives who reinforce our negative view of ourselves. Many times, these are the people closest to us, family and friends who don't see our potential. They latch onto and often encourage us to reinforce harmful behaviors in a manner that supports our limiting beliefs.

People who attempt to upload garbage to our software aren't in a place to know or accept our personal destiny or purpose. They have not lived our lives or walked in our shoes. They have not had our experiences, and they do not have our talents.

I encourage you to minimize (or better yet—eliminate) contact with naysayers and negative reinforcers as much as possible.

Instead, surround yourself with an inner circle of people who say, "I believe in you. You will find a way to make a violin out of an old, discarded pizza pan."

These people know who we are and will help us to stand strong in our power.

The Power of Our "Why"

It's important to recognize that we all hold a story. The movie we "star in" can either keep us back or provide motivation and inspiration to become more. Take my friend Marissa Nehlsen, who was one of eight children living in poverty; today, she is the founder of an incredibly successful financial investing firm, Freedom Financial Group.

Marissa's mother lived for many years in an abusive marriage. When Marissa was a teenager, her mom woke the children in the middle of the night. "Come on, kids. We're leaving and not coming back."

Now a single mother with no place to live and no financial support, Marissa's mother moved the family into a rundown two-bedroom trailer house in North Dakota. Their only source of heat was a small kerosene heater. Old blankets were nailed over the doors and windows during the bitterly cold winters to keep the heat from escaping the drafty trailer. The nine of them would huddle together on a bedraggled brown sofa they salvaged from a dumpster to keep warm.

Even now, Marissa remembers that old couch, the freezing winters, and the blankets lining the doors and windows. When she was fifteen, it finally dawned on her that her family was living in abject poverty. Shocked and stunned by the reality of their circumstances, Marissa looked at her mother and said, "Mom, we're those people they talk about on TV. We're not just poor, we're ridiculously poor, we're crazy poor."

Marissa remembers her mother's response to this day. She looked squarely at her daughter and said, "Yes, we are poor, Marissa, but you can choose to be a victim, or you can be victorious. It is a choice. What are you going to choose?"

Though she only said it that one time, Marissa's mother's words deeply resonated with her daughter, becoming her mantra when she faced a challenge.

Fast forward four years. At nineteen, Marissa found herself pregnant. She recognized that she had made some poor choices, and her mom's words came to mind. "You can be a victim, or you can be victorious." She knew that she didn't want her child to grow up in poverty, living in a decrepit mobile home warmed by a toxic kerosene heater.

Marissa had purpose; she had a compelling "why"—her newborn daughter. She focused on graduating from high school, and when presented with an opportunity to turn five dollars into financial freedom, she took it.

Her aunt was in the insurance business, and she gave the young mother a chance. Marissa recalled a quote from Zig Ziglar that said, "If you help enough people get what they want, you can get what you want." She realized if she embraced the mindset of helping others, she could also help herself.

Marissa's aunt gave her the chance she needed. She told her she would pay her five dollars for every new client appointment she set. "I ended up making sixty dollars a day doing that—which was a really good gig. From that point on, I knew whatever obstacle came my way, I would choose to overcome it. I would choose victory."

Her mother instilled in her the seed of choosing who she wanted to be. She knew she didn't want to be poor or broke. She didn't want to live in the same trailer park for the rest of her life. She didn't want to raise her baby in the same harsh, hard environment in which she had grown up. She didn't want to be a victim—she wanted to be victorious.

Marissa was determined to do something different to get something different.

Today, Marissa runs an extremely successful financial services organization, which she built from the basement of her home. She continually reiterates the importance of our thoughts, "It is vital to recognize the pitfall of the thoughts we think and words we say.

If we can change our mind, we can change our entire life and the lives of everyone around us. It is in this space in our mind that either makes us a victim or a victor."

Mindset starts with being aware of what you are telling yourself about who you are.

CHAPTER FOUR

Power and Influence

After studying power from a research standpoint and coming up with ideas on using power that seemed like they had practical implications, I decided to experiment. I began applying the *Power Up Power Down* techniques strategically in my own life, and upon seeing successful results, I coached others to implement these same methods. There were profound changes in self-empowerment and relationships across the board. The pieces of the power puzzle were becoming clear.

And like finding the "corner puzzle pieces," it all came together when I attended a training by Dr. Robert Cialdini, author and renowned expert for his work on *Influence* and *Pre-suasion*. He has spent his career over the last thirty years conducting scientific research on what leads people to say "Yes."

Dr. Cialdini is known globally as the expert in the science of ethical influence and how to apply it in business. His six Principles of Persuasion—reciprocity, liking, scarcity, consistency, authority, and consensus—are universal and can be taught and learned.

After completing one of his programs, I decided to pursue becoming a Cialdini Method Certified Trainer. This was a huge undertaking and no easy task. It included hundreds of hours of study time, oral and written exams, one-on-one coaching, and rigorously audited presentations of the material. (Only thirteen people are presently credentialed to teach the Principles of Persuasion, and I'm honored to be the only woman certified in the US.)

Armed with this new knowledge, I finally understood how influence and power fit together—and how effective that combination is. I was able to take what I had learned from Stanford University, John Maxwell, and Dr. Cialdini and interpret their collective teachings from a female perspective.

The influence principles integrate with power and give us choice. It's all about knowing which persuasion principle and/or power move to use and how to use them ethically and appropriately.

Again, this bears repeating: Using influence and power properly is not about controlling others to do what you want them to do despite their resistance. That is not power or influence; that is hierarchy and dominance. Nobody wins in that type of situation.

Effective and ethical use of power is about mutual empowerment.

In his book *Influence*, Dr. Cialdini says:

"Much of the compliance process (wherein one person is spurred to comply with another person's request) can be understood in terms of the human tendency for automat-

ic shortcut responding. Most individuals in our culture have developed a set of trigger features for compliance, that is, as a set of specific pieces of information that normally tell us when compliance with a request is likely to be correct and beneficial."

In other words, we have a set of responses to any given situation. Most of these responses reside in our unconscious and were either developed as a learned behavior over time or were reinforced by other people or circumstances.

Typically, automatic responses or "triggers" are small subtle signs, people, situations, actions, or words that cause us to react with little to no conscious thought. They can be emotional or psychologically based. These responses can be beneficial when they help us easily navigate through the vast number of choices we are required to make every day, such as when we see a "sale" sign while searching for a good deal.

However, some triggers can also hinder us, especially when we are talking about personal interactions, just like yelling as a child doesn't serve us well in adulthood. Having awareness of our personal triggers helps us to respond appropriately to any given situation.

Even though it is a natural tendency to react with a raised voice when someone is yelling at you, in order to have influence, it is much more productive to respond to the trigger/stimulus (in this case, the yelling) in an entirely different manner. This method of enhancing the use of influence can strengthen the relationship and create forward movement. This is at our disposal by choosing whether we Power Up or Power Down.

By becoming more aware of the potential that lies between any given stimulus and how to respond, it changes our influence with others. Fortunately, when we change the way we respond, we can improve the interaction experience for all involved.

Kate's "Goldilocks Dilemma"

As an executive coach, I often have the opportunity to coach women on the best ways to advance their careers. Kate was one of these women. She held a director of fundraising position in a healthcare system and wanted to move her career to the next level.

Despite her pleasing demeanor and expertise, Kate was faced with the Goldilocks Dilemma: Her appearance and likability overshadowed all of her other attributes. The Goldilocks Dilemma, as revealed in the article "The Goldilocks Dilemma: Why Career Advancement Is So Much Harder for Women than Men and What Women Can Do to Change That" by Andie & Al, can be a problem many women face. Studies conducted by Catalyst Research and social psychologist Amy Cuddy have shown that women are considered competent or likable at work but rarely both.

Extremely intelligent and personable, Kate had a knack of knowing the best way to approach people, build rapport, and gain trust. Everyone who met Kate liked her instantly. She was friendly, genuine, and outgoing. She was also accomplished at her job, raising funds far beyond her goal for the health system.

Although her boss would praise her publicly, stating how lucky the foundation was to have her, she felt her talent, proficiency, and contributions were often overlooked.

I urged Kate to have an open conversation with her boss, Nathan, asking him the precise steps she needed to take to move up the organizational ranks. She was reluctant but realized her hesitance was based on her fear of potential confrontation.

Kate's heart raced as she proceeded to his office for the scheduled meeting. As she took a seat, Kate realized that it was suddenly quite warm in the office, making her all the more uncomfortable as she crossed and uncrossed her legs in the chair across from her manager. She was scared that she might not have the nerve to ask her questions and worried Nathan might say she was just not good enough.

Taking a deep breath, Kate explained to Nathan that she wanted his advice on what was necessary to advance her career. He told her she possessed exceptional people skills, worked well with her team, and was liked by all. Just as she was feeling hopeful and began to let down her guard, he said, "You have a lot of incredible assets, Kate, and I value you very much. But there is one key thing holding you back. You need to increase your people and communication skills to effectively manage a team."

Although this contradicted what Nathan had just expressed to her, Kate didn't ask for clarification. Disheartened, she simply nodded, thanked him, and excused herself.

When I spoke with Kate a few days later, she was an emotional wreck. Her thoughts replayed a "You are not good enough" message that had sent her into an irrational tailspin.

Frustrated, confused, and demoralized, she had spent days trying to decipher what her boss was trying to say. As she shared the story of her meeting, it became evident that Kate needed to intentionally move out of the role she had unconsciously chosen on the power continuum.

This was going to take some work on her part. First, she needed to reprogram some of her limiting beliefs. Over her lifetime, Kate's inner voice had whispered things to her that weren't true but that she now had internalized.

"You don't matter. You will never be a leader. No one looks up to you. What do you really know, anyway? Oh, Kate, you aren't as smart as you think you are. All that stuff you know doesn't mean anything."

These unconscious and insidious self-imposed limiting beliefs held Kate back and pushed her down. They kept her from growing, from taking valid critiques from others and using them to better herself. They kept her from correcting the people who interrupted her because she always felt what she had to say couldn't be as important as what they were sharing.

The first step to regaining our power always starts with our belief system and the thoughts we allow to play in our head. To move forward, Kate needed to reframe what she was telling herself about who she was and what she could accomplish.

She chose a powerful self-affirmation to replace the whisperings of that niggling, negative voice. When it began murmuring in her ear, she would cut it off and say to herself, "I am a person of value. I have things to add that others are unable to because they are not me." Next, Kate had to become conscious of what her movements, speech, and behaviors were communicating. It was more natural to her to be friendly, allow others to speak, and sit quietly by. But this was a barrier to Kate's influence.

Initially, Kate felt awkward as she learned how to use speech, nonverbal cues, and behaviors to increase her power. But Kate's subtle verbal and nonverbal changes began to pay off.

About two weeks later, Kate and Nathan were hosting some volunteers for dinner to gather insights on moving forward with a project. Nathan had asked her to attend, telling her how much he valued her strategic ideas.

When they arrived at the restaurant, Kate discovered that she was the only female in attendance—the entire assembly of volunteers was men. As the group was seated, Kate and Nathan ended up sitting close to one other. Nathan proceeded to welcome everyone and made a point to introduce Kate. But then he slipped, jokingly saying Kate was at the meeting to take notes.

Kate was appalled and upset. Instantly, her face flushed, and her body tensed. Feeling belittled and devalued, questions swarmed in her mind. How could she correct her boss in front of all these men and still keep her dignity? He had asked her to accompany him to this critical meeting, so how could he sabotage her role at the meeting with such a statement?

As anger started to well up inside her, she remembered our discussion about Powering Up and Powering Down. She decided to respond by Powering Up instead of reacting.

Kate smiled at the group, tilting her head back slightly. With a calm voice, she addressed the group slowly with intentional pauses. "Yes, that is correct. I will be taking notes since I'll be spearheading the strategy for this project. Please speak up so I can hear you and allow me the grace to interrupt you for clarity so that I can make sure this project is successful."

Kate did interrupt throughout dinner, made eye contact, and leaned back in her chair.

The next morning, Nathan called her into his office.

"Kate, I just wanted to tell you how impressed I was with your performance last night… It is high time to think about promoting you."

CHAPTER FIVE

Power-full Boundaries

Setting and adhering to boundaries is a common issue, and many women struggle with boundaries on a daily basis; maintaining proper boundaries requires constant vigilance. It is a misconception to think boundaries only affect our personal life. Lack of appropriate boundaries in the workplace can account for fear, mistrust, escalating conflict, and a general dissatisfaction within a team and one's overall job satisfaction.

"No" is a seemingly simple word. As young children, no was a word we used frequently. Toddlers often defiantly say no to their parents but quickly discover that word is not acceptable. As we get older, it seems that many of us carry that toddler interaction into our belief system: Saying no is inappropriate and impolite. I believe this is why so many of us have struggled with saying it and setting proper personal boundaries at some point or another in our lives.

The Definition of Boundaries

Boundaries are rules that a person creates to identify reasonable, safe, and permissible ways for other people to behave toward them and also defines how they will respond should those limits be breached.

To define boundaries in a visual context, think about a backyard. Every person who owns a home is responsible for their own backyard and its upkeep. We landscape, water, plant flower beds, and mow the grass. Even if we don't do the work ourselves, we employ someone else to take care of this space. We create a place to sit, entertain, and maybe barbecue. Most of us like nothing more than to gather outside in our backyards with family or friends, enjoying a good meal and conversation.

I remember growing up as a child in the Midwest; there were only a few months of great weather to enjoy the backyard, so we cherished every opportunity. Weekends and many weeknights were filled with my father caring for our yard to ensure it was perfect for our family to get maximum pleasure out of it. He even (bravely) cleared a wooded area at the edge of our property that was covered with poison ivy because I was extremely allergic. It took a lot of hard work and diligence on his part to keep our yard beautiful.

I remember my father meticulously removing unwanted rocks from our yard. He did this for two reasons, one to make the yard attractive and the other to make sure the smaller rocks didn't get caught in the lawnmower and shoot out the side, hurting someone or damaging something. He knew that small rocks could cause harm. My father had no tolerance for rocks in his yard and spent a lot of time and effort seeking them out to dispose of them.

My father also knew where the property line started and where it ended. He groomed right up to the edges of our property line, and our neighbor did the same up to his. If anyone else looked at the two yards, they would not be able to tell where the property lines were, but my family and our neighbors knew exactly where each one was.

Dr. Henry Cloud has the reputation of being a world-renowned expert on boundaries. I had the privilege to hear him speak twenty-some years ago and have followed his work ever since. His work has provided me with valuable insight into my daily life and how my lack of setting proper boundaries has caused me many headaches over the years. Understanding boundaries has enabled me to identify how I have, on occasion, handed my power away.

In fact, one of the things he said really hit home with me, "Knowing what I am to own and take responsibility for gives me freedom. If I know here is where my yard begins and ends, I am free to do with it what I like. Taking responsibility for my life opens up many different options. However, if I do not 'own' my life, my choices and options become very limited."

Visualizing my childhood yard helped me understand Dr. Cloud's concept of boundaries as property lines. It's extremely important to be aware of our boundaries and where our responsibility starts and ends. On almost a daily basis, we encounter people who want us to take responsibility for them or their actions, whether that be a work assignment, responsibility for a decision they have made, or even their own emotions.

In these instances, it is vital to muster the courage to hold steady to our personal boundaries and say no politely. Occasionally, we will encounter people who refuse to hear us or attempt to bulldoze over our established limitations. But empowerment requires us to have the ability to set boundaries, say no, and uphold that decision as well as respecting the boundaries of others.

Having our own set of clear personal boundaries is much like a yard; it is essential to know where our boundaries begin and where they end. Setting protections around them, just like a fence protects and defines a yard, delineates what is our responsibility and deflects what belongs to others. An awareness of vital personal parameters is important in determining if the situation at hand is a boundary or power issue.

Just as my father was diligent in our backyard, if someone throws their "rock" over our "fence," we might need to politely toss it back.

Dr. Cloud teaches the critical nature of establishing physical, mental, emotional, and spiritual limits to distinguish what is our responsibility and what isn't. This defines "what is me" (my property and my responsibility) and "what is not me" (not my property or responsibility).

Boundaries are not meant to be impenetrable walls to withdraw behind, keeping us isolated and alone. Far from it. Our personal limits help us own our life, giving us a specific sense of ownership. Healthy boundaries keep the good in (like our self-worth) and the bad out (such as manipulation using guilt or fear).

Our personal boundaries are invisible to others but always present, like the property lines in our backyards. Outsiders will not always know where our personal boundaries begin or end. This is why it is important to clearly define, openly communicate, actively defend, and continually maintain personal boundary property lines.

Firmly held boundaries guide us in holding our personal power, which consists of our attitudes, behavior, beliefs, values, choices, talents, thoughts, and desires. Boundaries enable us to hold steady and not continuously relinquish our property lines, acquiesce our responsibility, and hand over our personal power to others.

The foundation of achieving personal power is *through* the establishing and maintaining of our boundaries. Then and only then can we use our talents to the fullest and live our purpose.

Internal and External Pressures

As with all things in life, we will always encounter pressure to allow someone to cross our property line or let go of the boundary power established. This influence to relinquish our boundary power comes in two forms: internal and external forces.

Internal pressures are those placed on ourselves, which coerces us to go against our idea of what should be done. This can stem from our limiting self-beliefs or feelings of guilt or obligation that we've accepted or placed upon ourselves.

These internal forces are strong motivators for many of us when setting aside our self-imposed personal limits. Fear of anger, unresolved loss/grief, fear of the unknown, change, guilt, and abandonment are reasons one might discard boundary limits. Many of these causes are a result of self-limiting beliefs or messages reinforced in relationships or past situations.

External pressure comes from others telling or persuading us about what to do or how to act. Both can be strong influencers and, at times, are valid and deserve our consideration. But often, these pressures are ways in which we either self-sabotage or allow other people to exert control over the power we've created to safeguard our "personal property lines."

People tend to look externally for the source of a problem. It is easier to look to others to blame than to take responsibility. But pointing the finger at other people for our lack of boundary power places us in a state of being the victim. This outlook leaves us with powerless blame; we are at the mercy of others, unable to effect change in our own lives or use power.

For those of us who've accepted last-minute projects, taken on more responsibility with no recognition or additional compensation, or said yes when you really wanted to say no, these feelings could be your "property line" alarm bells ringing.

The Boundary Buster

Several years ago, Fred, a good friend of mine, worked for Samantha, a very successful businesswoman. Samantha was smart, determined, and hardworking. But while she was an adamant protector of her own boundaries, she was a notorious boundary buster to others.

Samantha and Fred became acquainted through their sons, who had become friends in first grade. They would bump into one another at school functions and would chat during playdate drop-offs and pick-ups. A few years after their initial association, Samantha recruited Fred to work for her as she built her business. Almost instantly, respect of Fred's personal time was brought to an abrupt end. She began calling and texting Fred at all hours, including early mornings, evenings, and weekends, with "urgent" work requests.

One Monday morning, Fred was dropping his son off at her house so their boys could walk to school together. He had been working on another urgent project Samantha had given him and had some questions about how to proceed. They were standing outside with their morning coffee and after a few minutes of conversation, he took the initiative to ask her for some clarification on a work-related issue.

Immediately, her eyes narrowed, and her lips thinned into a hard line. As she glared at him, he could feel anger coming off of her in palpable waves.

"How DARE you come to my home and encroach upon my personal time by asking me about work outside of the workday?" Samantha snapped.

Fred was shocked and speechless. He had falsely assumed that since Samantha felt comfortable sending business his way during non-work hours, he was also free to make an "after-hours" inquiry. Just the day before, which was Sunday, she had contacted him to work on this same project saying that it was a top priority.

Fred was taken aback from this unexpected comment and her strong reaction to his question. After some consideration he stated, "I am so sorry, Samantha. I know that this project is important, and thought since I was here, I'd ask you about it so I could hit the ground running once I got into the office."

"Well, you thought wrong. Don't you ever do that again," Samantha firmly stated. Not knowing how to respond, he said he would see her later at the office and left.

As he drove away, he mentally replayed all of the times she had encroached on his boundaries around non-work hours and responded to her request without fail.

As Fred was telling me this story, he recalled an instance on a Saturday morning when Samantha called to assign him a new client project due on Monday. She implied that whatever he was doing wasn't as important as "making this project happen." It appeared to not matter to her when Fred told her that he had plans with his family and that she was asking him to break his plans. She even went so far as to say she would remember Fred's unwillingness to serve this client when it was time for raises. Fred felt he had no choice but to complete this project on this very tight deadline.

Furthermore, to make this project a reality, he had to contact vendors and coworkers during their personal weekend time to request their urgent assistance.

Samantha had a habit of creating crises by promising clients unreasonable deadlines and then offloading her responsibility to Fred. She was an expert at causing undue stress on Fred and the team by assigning tasks during their personal time off.

Fred began feeling extremely unappreciated and disrespected for his extra efforts as Samantha continued to call him after hours with urgent work requests. As time went on, Fred became more and more stressed, angry, and even resentful. And, not surprisingly, so did his family. He made every attempt to communicate boundaries, but Samantha seemed to refuse to hear and/or accept them.

After putting up with her blatant disregard around personal boundaries, Fred finally had enough. The last straw came immediately following a candid conversation with her and her business partner about this continual boundary-busting. Despite assurances that this "would not happen again," Samantha texted him at 8 a.m. the very next morning, which was a holiday.

Realizing that her behavior was never going to change, Fred submitted a letter of resignation. Even after the letter, Samantha continued her boundary-busting behavior. She left numerous desperate voicemails and sent multiple text messages saying how much Fred had upset her.

Nowhere in any of her messages was an acknowledgment that she had encroached on Fred's personal boundaries. Although Fred had raised his concerns with her numerous times over the last six months and explicitly spelled out in his resignation letter exactly why he was leaving, Samantha remained oblivious to her boundary-busting behavior that caused his departure. She even tried to play the victim with Fred, saying that he was leaving her "high and dry" by not bringing the project to completion in an attempt to guilt him. Luckily, Fred had finally learned the importance of holding true to his personal boundaries and was not swayed by her tactics.

Setting and sticking to boundaries is not always easy. For Fred it was a slippery slope, and he should have never let it go as long as he did. He confessed to me later that it was fear that stood in the way of him standing up for himself.

But ultimately, he did finally come to the realization that he was the one who needed to take his power back, establish his boundaries, and reclaim his self-respect and self-worth.

CHAPTER SIX

Maintaining Your Power Boundaries

D r. Henry Cloud's words bear repeating: "Boundaries define us. They define what is me and what is not me. A boundary shows me where I end and someone else begins, leading me to a sense of ownership. Knowing what I am to own and take responsibility for gives me freedom."

Maintaining our power with firm boundaries in the workplace is essential but can also be very tricky. It can be challenging to protect our limits in an environment where we feel obliged when we are asked by an authority figure to do something. But someone who understands boundaries will never purposefully encroach upon the limits of others and will accept a polite but firm no.

Just like Fred, a lack of limits from the get-go openly enabled Samantha to be overly intrusive and created a situation in which he could never recover. Likewise, setting boundaries that are too fluid or permeable may keep us and others from owning responsibilities and, in many cases, siphons away our personal power.

Defining and holding firm to boundary limits from the outset enables us to be better equipped to stand in our power. But that can't happen if we don't identify what our boundaries are.

Many of us take on the responsibilities of our managers' or coworkers' lack of planning and fail to set limits out of fear. We are afraid that if we stand up to someone in a position of authority, we could lose our job, be overlooked for a promotion, be branded as a problematic employee, or we may just have a deeply ingrained fear or belief around having boundaries at all.

Establishing our personal "property lines" is critical to our well-being. We may have slightly different boundaries at work and in our personal lives, but those limits are nonetheless vital.

In a remote work environment, it can be especially challenging to set boundaries because you are not there in person and have to respond many times via email or even via text. I encourage you to use warm but firm words in your responses. Email is very tricky and, if not done correctly, can send the wrong message.

Setting proper boundaries in email or in text becomes easier over time. Following the below guidelines can help in the journey:

- Never write the email while emotional. Your response is important and requires a clear head to craft the proper reply.
- Take time in responding. Email and text have a way of making us think there is a need to respond in the moment. It is okay to not reply immediately. In fact, having a delayed response is a way of establishing boundaries.

- When your emotions have settled, draft your response email, walk away, and come back later to read it with fresh eyes.
- Don't apologize or over-explain. Be polite, succinct, and firm.
- If you have the opportunity, have someone you trust look at your response before you send it, especially when the topic can be emotionally charged.
- Sometimes following up with a phone call after the email or text is sent can be beneficial. It takes more time, but it can go a long way in the relationship to make sure the message was not misunderstood.

Taking time to do the work needed to ensure boundaries are well defined, communicated, and defended will serve us well. If this topic of boundaries is a completely new concept to you, keep in mind that it is a process and does get easier with practice.

Taking a personal boundary inventory is a good first place to start.

For those moving into a new position, joining a new team or company, set boundaries from the outset. Make limits clear and inform others of what to expect from you should those boundaries be breached. For example, "I will not do work after hours, and if you want me to, it will take advance notice and mutual consent."

For those individuals who have been in a job where their boundaries were usurped or blurred, it's time to regain power. It can be scary to stand up for ourselves, but in the long run, we will have more respect for ourselves and respect from others.

How to Safeguard Boundaries

Boundaries require diligent communication and defense. Some people are so adept at circumventing our limits that we unconsciously consent to their continual boundary-busting behavior. This conduct can occur in the workplace, with friends or social groups, and in family situations.

Imagine this situation. It's Friday at 4:45 p.m. Your coworker, Meg, either rushes or saunters into your office and sits on the corner of your desk.

"Hey, I'm glad I caught you before you left for the weekend. The project that's due on Monday, well, I could use your help. I got slammed this week with a client issue and didn't have time to pull together the slide deck for the presentation to management. I immediately thought of your amazing PowerPoint skills. Since you've bailed me out of situations before, I knew you would have my back. It shouldn't take more than an hour or so. I would do it, but I'm going out of town this weekend."

The real situation: Your colleague's poor planning (and her desire to keep her weekend plans) is like throwing a rock into your backyard by asking you at the last minute to take work home that isn't your responsibility.

- **Ask yourself:** How does this make you feel? Maybe you feel guilty not taking on work others ask you to do. Will you say yes outwardly but be internally resentful?
- **Examine the symptom:** Are you saying yes to the rock that has been thrown into your yard? Or is this something that you truly want to say yes to?
- **Identify the root cause:** What in your past or childhood taught you to accept the rock? Were other people (family, friends) asking you to help them out of binds they'd got-

ten themselves into and, if you didn't, they threatened to withdraw their affections?

- **Identify the need:** Fear of abandonment? Guilt? What is it that is causing you to allow this person to step all over your boundaries and allow you to give your power away?
- **Respond, don't react:** Take a deep breath to "collect yourself." Then respond with something like, "Meg, it sounds like you had a tough week with that unexpected client problem. I understand you are in a tight spot, but I won't be able to help you. This project is your responsibility, not mine. I'd be happy to help next time if you ask at least two workdays in advance."

If you have helped Meg in the past in similar situations, she may balk at your sudden hardline stance. Don't let any bullying or threats deter you from holding firm. Continue to empathize without acquiescing.

"I understand this is stressful for you. How else can I help other than doing the slides for you during my personal time?"

Clear, open communication is the foundation of healthy boundary-setting. Limits can be communicated in a variety of ways to maintain our self-power. Below are some things to consider when establishing and communicating the power of boundaries.

- Verbalize clearly with words what your boundaries are.
- Visualize your boundaries as your backyard property line.
- Graciously throw the rock back over the fence: "I'm sorry, but that is not going to work for me."
- Identify those who continually try to break through your boundaries and put distance between you and that person when possible.

Standing firm in our boundaries gets easier over time and boundary-busters will eventually realize we are not easy prey.

And remember, it's okay to take baby steps. The goal is progress, not perfection!

The Difference Between Boundaries and Power

Boundaries are the "special sauce" in interpersonal power, but there is a distinct difference between power and boundaries. We must know, understand, and hold on to boundaries in order to choose the proper role in power.

Maintaining our boundary power allows us to maintain a yard we can be proud of and thoroughly enjoy. Much like keeping a yard or garden, there is work involved. There is no way to give the best of ourselves in the workplace and life if we do not hold on to our self-power through boundaries.

There is a reason self-love, self-respect, and self-worth all start with the word "self." These are all deserving gifts we owe to ourselves. Therefore, holding our boundaries is first and foremost to stepping into and maintaining our self-power.

Boundaries are an essential aspect of power. When we hold firm to our personal limits, we are defining and establishing our true empowerment. We also show the world where we will and will not be moved.

For example, if you have decided not to work from home in the evenings or on weekends, and you ask people not to call or text you after 6 p.m., if you answer incoming calls or texts, you are allowing them to push through your boundary. No matter how hard or uncomfortable it feels, it is important that you define the limits and stick to them. You might need to turn off your phone or put it in sleep mode to hold tight to a 6 p.m. shut-off time.

Often to our own detriment, we tend to confuse boundaries and power. Simply put, boundaries are the limits we set around our time, energy, and money. They identify our personal responsibilities and ensure we do not accept the responsibilities of others.

Healthy, defined boundaries give us confidence. They give us freedom to truly allow ourselves and others to have a voice, be heard, and cultivate trust in relationships. When you are able to stand in your power, others are given the ability to do the same.

CHAPTER SEVEN

Power Personalities

S o, let's take a break from talking about some of the heavier issues around power and have some fun!

Through my years in leadership positions and coaching, there have been various situations that have risen to the surface around power. They cross generations, positions, gender, cultures, and industries.

Six personality types stand out, and every organization, no matter how great, has at least one.

I have taken some creative license and named these six situations/personalities to better identify them. I'll explain each one in detail as we go but they are:

1. The Toxic Pollinator
2. The Snaker

3. The Insulter-Offloader
4. The InfoHoarder
5. The Negatron
6. The Swoop and Poop

Now, if we're being honest, we may recognize ourselves as being one of these types at some point in time. In fact, we may have even been the catalyst! If you have been a part of instigating or propagating these situations, don't beat yourself up. Instead, the goal is to heighten our awareness and move forward, making better choices in the future by using our power properly.

But just like the junkyard orchestra, we can take the situation and do our best to make beautiful music moving forward. There will always be occasions when, despite our best efforts, we can't effect positive change. If we have done all we can to make inroads or forward progress in a toxic situation, sometimes there is no option but to remove ourselves from it.

In the workplace, we frequently have difficult interactions time and again, but if we attach the word negotiation to these exchanges, the hair on the back of our neck stands up. What we often miss is that negotiation is a natural part of social interactions; viewing it as such takes away its intimidation factor.

Over time, as I have encountered these personalities, I have arrived at a better understanding of how to employ negotiation and power principles to transform them into a positive outcome.

These principles include having clear boundaries, a solid and positive personal belief system, and being genuinely inquisitive. I've taken Dr. Cialdini's six Principles of Persuasion—reciprocity, liking, scarcity, consistency, authority, and consensus—and applied them to these "caricatures" of people and situations we encounter in the workplace.

CHAPTER EIGHT

The Toxic Pollinator

When I was consulting for a not-for-profit foundation, they needed help reducing conflicts in their team meetings. Everyone was continually getting upset, and ultimately the work was not being accomplished to the level it could have been.

To get a better understanding of the dynamics at play, I asked if I could sit in on the meetings. At first, I sat quietly, observing the behaviors of the people present. It didn't take long to see that Charlie had little to say in the meetings.

In one particular forum, Charlie sat back for the majority of the meeting. But when the topic came up about distributing job assignments for a team member who had left the organization just before a hiring freeze, he was quick to jump in to provide a solution.

I thought it odd that Charlie was the one who volunteered because the open position was so out of the scope of his wheelhouse. I remember thinking, "If it looks like a duck, it's probably a duck." But I had to be sure I was dealing with a Toxic Pollinator.

Several times a day, I began taking "reconnaissance" walks throughout the office, noticing who was meeting with whom. I would occasionally interrupt with a quick, "Just checking to see if I can be of any help." Sometimes the individuals would tell me what they were talking about, but most of the time they didn't. One common denominator I observed was that Charlie was engaging in tête-à-têtes with just about everyone. It seemed my intuition was correct.

I began taking detailed notes of things Charlie said to me alone, in team meetings, and even things others told me he said. Then I used these records strategically in meetings to draw Charlie into the conversation. I would interject something like, "Charlie, last week in our one-on-one meeting, you told me that, based on your assessment, we could get the work done without too much strain on any of us," or "Charlie, it's just like you said a few weeks ago. We have a very cooperative team and a great work environment here."

When he was sitting quietly, I would draw him out and ask his opinion and then, if possible, say, "Yes, I heard you told the same thing to Christy last week." Not only was I bringing up consistency to Charlie about what he was saying, but I was also offering up this information to the group, increasing power through consistent language. This public sharing made it difficult for him to retreat to negative talk with people in private when he was consistently quoted positively in meetings.

Much like a bee moves from flower to flower transferring pollen, seemingly unnoticed Toxic Pollinators use disharmony as their method of influence. Their covert mission is to create discord and mistrust among team members, coworkers, and close groups to deflect attention away from themselves and their underlying agenda. They are masters at cultivating an undercurrent that draws others in, manipulating situations to bring issues to the forefront without them having to do so personally.

These people buzz around pollinating rumors and half-truths to individuals or small groups. They thrive on inciting drama by sprinkling tidbits of information here and there. When all of the group members come together, such as in a business meeting, family reunion, or social gathering, the drama ignites and power is relinquished.

In a virtual or remote setting, this is still very common and often goes unnoticed for extended periods of time. I believe it is because this person can't be seen moving from office to office having conversations but instead is using text or email to have completely clandestine conversations. A Toxic Pollinator may be harder to spot in this situation, but if highly charged outcomes are occurring, then take a closer look and talk to people outside the meeting. Someone will eventually slip and say, "Charlie and I were talking…"

Toxic Pollinators want to gain others' trust, so they are meticulous and deliberate about how they pollinate. As a catalyst for organizational dissonance, they often go undetected for years. People are lured by their apparent friendliness, not realizing that by confiding in them, they are providing "insider information" that gives the Toxic Pollinator the power to inflame and create a dysfunctional culture. These drama drones quickly learn what buttons to push with key people, manipulating conversations by disseminating provocative information, knowing the individuals involved will inadvertently do their dirty work.

The task of a Toxic Pollinator is to foster emotionally charged situations. If there is no obvious problem poised to implode, they will often create a situation by making something up. They thrive on getting people riled up, and when things get heated, they fuel the fire by continuing to pollinate misinformation and half-truths. They love to do this when there is a business situation or issue that people are passionate about, especially if views are opposing. When the flames are at their peak, the Toxic Pollinator flies in to put out the fire and save the day, often volunteering to take on a vital task. Not only do they create the drama, but they also orchestrate the ensuing theatrics so they come out looking like the hero(ine).

Toxic Pollinators flit from person to person, creating discord as their method of influence.

Identifying a Toxic Pollinator

Toxic Pollinators are inconsistent. They revise and change their story and the information they share depending on the person with whom they are communicating. One of the best ways to make sure you have correctly identified them is by keeping detailed notes on what they've said, when, and to whom. This process will help you recognize the variability of their facts.

Things to help identify a Toxic Pollinator include:

- People who have many sidebar conversations with one or two people at a time, especially behind closed doors.
- Individuals who have very little to say in group settings.
- Those who never address or broach issues directly in a group or meeting.
- People who always appear calm and very quiet in the middle of conflict.
- Individuals who have no stake in the game and remain neutral when a meeting blows up.
- Those who constantly seem to "save the day."

Thanks to the smoke screen designed to spotlight them as the superhero, Toxic Pollinators frequently go undetected. The drama they ignite can allow a culture of dysfunction to flourish within the team and/or organization for years.

Teams and groups learn to operate around Toxic Pollinators. If the Pollinator is removed or leaves, someone else on the team will often unconsciously step into the role, continuing that individual's destructive dynamic because drama has created a habit the team is accustomed to functioning within.

The next time you find yourself in the middle of an overheated group, look around to see if you can spot someone sitting quietly. If you do, that doesn't mean they are a Toxic Pollinator; some people are naturally more reserved and may not be prone to excitement or feel comfortable jumping into a group conversation. To be certain that someone is a Toxic Pollinator, talk with members of the group separately and ask if they have spoken to anyone else about the heated issue. If several people mention the same person, you may have a Toxic Pollinator in your midst.

However, be *extremely* careful to only ask the question of people in the group. You want to find out if they have "talked to anyone else" and not get into the toxic discussion yourself, or you may unintentionally add to the dysfunction.

Minimizing Their Impact

The approach necessary to minimize the effects of a Toxic Pollinator is to change how we deal with them personally and in meetings.

This is the type of situation that requires a solid grasp on our emotions and standing in our power. This means Powering Up in a manner that doesn't cause adversarial situations or result in forward movement being gridlocked.

Addressing the information flow on an individual level is a critical step. Once you have identified a Toxic Pollinator, take the necessary precaution of NOT confiding any additional pertinent information to them. Cutting off their information source (i.e., their pollen) will curtail their ability to pollinate discord, affording the opportunity to implement a program to change the culture of the team or organization.

It is equally important to call on these individuals directly in meetings. Even if you are not leading the discussion, ask them for their thoughts. These pollinating people are extremely reluctant to speak up or offer their opinion directly in any forum. Using your power to direct non-confrontational questions or requesting their input in group settings draws them out of their pollinating pattern. It is vital to deter the Toxic Pollinator from using you as a carrier of their drama. It is equally imperative to have a heightened awareness around information shared by others—it very well may have been received from the Pollinator.

Finally, after these stop-gap measures are in place, it might be helpful to work on the culture of the team and/or organization as well. Through my years of leading and consulting, I have found the most effective way to accomplish this is through team building and values integration. The most important part of making a culture shift is ensuring the values of the organization are "lived out loud" in the daily work of each individual.

Use the Principle of Consistency

One of the best power approaches to handle a Toxic Pollinator is to remind them of their own words. If we look hard enough, we will hear them say positive things and catch them being supportive of individuals, the team, and the organization itself.

There are few things more powerful than helping to create a place for people to be positively consistent with what they have said or done previously.

Dr. Robert Cialdini teaches six Principles of Persuasion that, if used ethically and morally, are factors that can increase your influence with others. One of those principles that helps us deal with a Toxic Pollinator is consistency.

Consistency, in Dr. Cialdini's terms, means that once a person makes a choice or takes a stand, they will encounter personal and interpersonal pressure to behave in a manner in alignment with their previous actions.

So, here's something interesting that sheds some light on this. While I was receiving my certification in the Principles of Persuasion, I learned about a 1968 study done by a pair of Canadian psychologists, Knox and Inkster. The pair observed people placing bets at the racetrack. Surprisingly, they discovered that people placing bets on specific horses became much more confident in their horse's ability to win after they put money down on that horse. This finding was seen over and over and revealed that the confidence level in the bettors rose once they put money behind their decision. The odds of the horse winning hadn't changed, but in the eyes of the person who placed the wager, the chosen horse's chance of winning the race had increased significantly as soon as money was on the line.

Why are we more likely to believe that something has better odds once we make a decision to support it? Dr. Cialdini teaches that we've invested in the outcome, which happens deep within us, directing our actions with quiet power. Much like placing a bet on a horse, our internal and often unconscious desire to remain congruent increases our confidence in our previous decisions.

We talk ourselves into believing that what we have previously said or done is correct even if there is additional evidence pointing otherwise. If we have taken a stand, made a decision, or formed a belief, we do not feel the need or desire to change our minds and will go to great lengths to support our previous decisions and commitments.

Our need for consistency is a powerful defense mechanism against cognitive dissonance, which is a state of mental discomfort resulting from holding inconsistent thoughts, attitudes, values, or beliefs. The individuals betting on racehorses know the odds of winning aren't great, so to reduce their unease, they convince themselves that the horse they've chosen will cross the finish line first.

Dr. Cialdini asks an important question, "Once we realize that the power of consistency is formidable in directing human action, an important practical question immediately arises: How is that force engaged?" The answer is that we experience pressure to behave consistently with commitments we have made in the past, especially if they are made in a public forum.

It is fascinating that we humans will instinctively stick to a consistent pattern of thinking or feeling without so much as a thought that this behavior can, or should, be changed. This shortcut taps into our fast brain, where many of our snap judgments, beliefs, and decisions are formed.

Let's look at how this applies to a Pollinator, toxic or not. In this instance, power involves a subtle approach, which will avoid creating tension and enhance the relationship. Being blunt tends to put people on the defensive. We are trying to lessen the drama instead of creating more pressure that ignites into arguments.

Many Pollinators are so busy buzzing around that they often don't remember what they have said in previous meetings or encounters. However, whether they have forgotten or are simply changing their tune doesn't hamper your ability to tap into this "personal and interpersonal pressure." Take notes of exactly what the Pollinator has said. Find opportunities to work any positive comments identified into conversations, preferably in front of others. Furthermore, if we can get the Pollinator to write these things down, such as in an email, it ingrains the commitment. Be sure to share only complimentary items to avoid inadvertently reinforcing undesired behavior.

Pollinators rarely change their outward actions. Since they thrive on drama, they may continue buzzing here and there. But if you can guide their pollinating toward the positive by implementing the weapon of consistency, it might eventually turn into honey.

This also shifts our awareness and utilizes the use of power language through positive words.

Remember Charlie, the Toxic Pollinator? The small step of repeating and reinforcing positive comments shifted Charlie's outlook as well as the outlook of those around him. Power accessed through the principle of consistency changed the entire attitude of the team.

There is an old saying, "you catch more flies with honey than vinegar." By using consistency, the principle itself becomes the honey. Shifting the focus to previously stated positive comments, ideas, and interactions implements and redirects power.

Because much of our life is lived in the fast brain, we often aren't conscious of many of our judgments, ideas, values, and beliefs. By using the power of consistency, we can move these default behaviors, beliefs, and actions to the forefront, allowing us to heighten conscience awareness, which can drive change.

CHAPTER NINE

The Snaker

We all know people who are genuinely charming, likable, and the life of the party, and these folks are great fun, so we have to be careful not to jump to conclusions too quickly. But if you've encountered a super friendly, flirty person who appears more insidious and leaves a path of underlying discord in their wake, you may have uncovered what I call a Snaker.

On the surface, Snakers are incredibly charming and pleasant. These lighthearted jokers liberally shower others with compliments and are friends with everyone they meet. They disguise themselves as non-threatening team players. Snaker personalities are very much like Kaa in Disney's 1967 children's movie *The Jungle Book*. Kaa is a dangerous python who uses his alluring personality to trick the young boy, Mowgli, into trusting him.

Like in the movie, these "schmoozers" or "players" cozy up to people, making nice to get information. They are masterful at doing this whether they are meeting in person or working remotely.

Inappropriate Humor

Snakers often quietly slither through the grass in the workplace and in social and family settings, disguising their true ulterior motives with humor and a likable, lively personality.

But watch out! A Snaker is a master manipulator and will quickly bare their fangs and strike when you least expect it. Snakers tend to use "humor" to cover their fangs. Even when you're writhing on the ground after their deliberate attack, others won't believe that person could possibly have done such a thing, precisely because they are so fun and non-threatening.

Adept at stealing others' ideas and claiming them as their own, these individuals might start out using "we" when discussing an idea but will quickly start saying "I" to take the credit for themselves. And if you attempt to correct them, those fangs will come out!

Snakers use funniness and charm to lure others into sharing information and ideas they will then claim as their own.

"People pleasers" are frequently the unwitting victims of relinquishing their power to a Snaker. These individuals tend to be more open in their communication style, sharing their knowledge and ideas—maybe a little too freely—with people like Snakers, who will use it to their advantage.

These "fun-loving," fang-hiding folks use smoke and mirrors in the guise of friendship to hide their incompetence and lack of expertise. They often don't possess the skills or knowledge necessary to do their job effectively, so they lure others into sharing critical information or completing projects, manipulating the situation in a way that enables them to take credit.

I once had a coworker named Matt, a Snaker who was a new addition to our team. He quickly started injecting humor and sarcasm into team meetings. At first, the team didn't know how to respond as it was often inappropriate and disruptive. However, since some of it actually was funny, everyone just accepted his behavior. Before we knew it, he was having regular drinks and taking fun trips with the boss outside of work. I started to notice I had less access to my boss and began hearing the same complaints from my coworkers.

If something was brought up that needed to be discussed with the manager, he would say, "Well, if you don't get to see him, I'd be happy to bring it up to him when we are together outside of work." It wasn't until I overheard him say to a coworker, "I have the boss's ear, so if you need anything, just come to me" that I became suspicious.

Then the very next week in a meeting, Matt took my idea and presented it as his own and my boss went on to praise him in front of the group for such a great idea. This solidified my suspicion that he was a Snaker. (My boss never figured out why so many of his great employees moved on to other jobs or positions.)

Identifying a Snaker

Keep a watchful eye on people who seem overly friendly, ply others with saccharine compliments, and are always the life of the party.

These Snakers also have a "sixth sense" of who needs to have their ego boosted. Snakers will do this with anyone they feel needs it, including clients, upper management, people in the C-suite, and even your best friend. By using our power of intuition, we can tell when someone is truly sincere and outgoing rather than using extroversion and flattery as a tool to get ahead.

Snakers will often:

- Use the same "script" over and over; the meat of their conversations is rehearsed.
- Be exceptionally easygoing; they are typically the life of the party at work and at home.
- Tell jokes and use humor and sarcasm, even using off-color or inappropriate banter.
- Be overly charming to compensate for lacking knowledge or skills at their job.
- Appear to be team players and non-threatening yet frequently claim the ideas of others.
- Sense when someone is upset or frustrated and come to them as a friend and confidante, then use that information to their benefit.

Minimizing Their Impact

Once we suspect that an individual is a Snaker personality, we can further confirm our theory by testing them with a small piece of information. For example, look for a low (yet appealing) ROI idea in a project, one in which credit doesn't matter, and feed that concept to the would-be Snaker. If that person claims the idea as their own, we've likely confirmed the type of person with whom we are dealing.

Things to keep in mind when dealing with a Snaker:

- Be mindful of how much information is shared at work and with whom we share it.
- Keep emotions intact and in check. Snakers excel at reading emotions and body language.
- If something upsetting or frustrating happens at work, take a walk or step away to allow time to calm down.
- Vent frustrations only to someone you completely trust outside of work.

Once a Snaker realizes that we are no longer a source of valuable information, they will move on in search of another target. It is absolutely crucial to Power Down by maintaining a friendly demeanor with a Snaker to avoid retaliation and retain a working relationship.

Even when this person is no longer sourcing us for ideas and crucial details, it is still crucial to be mindful of how meetings are held when a Snaker is involved. Sharing ideas and thoughts is vital to brainstorming and innovative ideas but be aware that Snakers will continue to hijack worthwhile, high-ROI concepts.

To neutralize this possibility, hold your power and present your ideas in meetings where many people are present so that a large group hears them. Before the meeting, consider detailing thoughts and ideas in an email sent to the entire cohort and, if appropriate, copy the manager. Both of these amicable strategies help curtail Snakers from stealing our ideas and taking credit for our creativity.

It's probably not surprising, but Snakers are fun to be around! It is perfectly acceptable to enjoy their entertaining, friendly personalities. But it is crucial to always be on guard to avoid falling into their snake pit. If we do, we may have difficulty getting back out.

Snakers are subtle in their undermining behaviors. Because of their carefully crafted buddy-buddy personality, no one suspects them, which means others won't believe we have been bitten, even if they've been a victim themselves. A Snaker tries to get the credit and the promotion; there is no use protesting or attempting to prove they falsely claimed our idea or weaseled their way into a position for which someone else is more qualified.

The key to holding on to your personal power with Snakers at work, or in even in your personal life, is to not fall victim to their flattery. It is tempting to be envious of their popularity. Understand that simply because they are well-liked doesn't mean they aren't knowledgeable. But by focusing on doing the best job we can at work, managing our emotions, and only sharing important information with those we trust or in large groups, we can beat the Snaker at their own game.

Use the Principle of Consensus

When dealing with a Snaker, use the power of consensus/social proof as a source of influence.

Let's imagine for a moment that we are traveling to a city we've never been to before and we're looking for a good steak restaurant. Pulling out our phone, we ask Siri for a list. Ten restaurants pop up within walking distance. How do we decide which one to go to?

Most of us look at rating stars or Yelp reviews. The more stars or higher the reviews mean others have had a good experience dining there. The place with over 500 reviews and five stars usually wins out over the one with fifty reviews and three stars.

People use consensus to decide what's appropriate to do in a situation by examining what others are doing.

Most larger companies have mission, vision, and values as part of their policy. At the very least, they will have a code of conduct. Whether the organization's values are written or not, the employees know what acceptable behavior is. It is essential to avoid finger-pointing and work toward creating a consensus that is brought to the attention of—and eventually bought into—by everyone.

The best use of power I've ever seen of creating consensus around a project was a community trying to increase volunteering. A couple of prominent members of the community started a foundation that gave college scholarships to high school students. The scholarships were not based on academic performance but instead on community service in the area. It didn't take long for students and community members alike to come together to support this endeavor. They even created additional consensus by providing awards to people and corporations that went above and beyond in the community. Every year, they have seen a steady increase in participation and volunteers from students, local residents, and companies.

This power of a consensus-building program could be easily replicated within an organization by rewarding people for important qualities such as teamwork, promoting others, and positive attitude attributes. The reward doesn't have to be something big. It can be a simple, symbolic gesture such as a rotating trophy or a bag of chocolates to the recipients.

I once worked as the president of a hospital foundation and needed the help of the board members to create awareness within the local community of fundraising opportunities. They were all supportive of the idea but not actively engaged.

I went to a local chocolatier and had them make big chocolate lips wrapped in shiny red foil much like the ones available on Valentine's Day. I would hand these out at each board meeting as a "Thanks for the lip service" award. (Playfulness can be a powerful strategy.) I've never seen so many people vying for chocolate! What this did was create a consensus of what each and every board member should be doing on a regular basis.

It becomes very challenging for a Snaker to survive in this type of atmosphere where everybody agrees on appropriate behavior and calls it out. Even if an organization isn't willing to implement such a creative program, we can use our personal power to create consensus by doing small things for people around us who excel and display positive qualities that need to be encouraged.

There are organizations where bad behavior has been happening for so long that nobody knows how to recover. Even in these environments, consensus is a powerful tool.

When using the power of consensus, it is crucial to establish shared core values, principles, and beliefs.

Everyone can become more aware of their actions, reactions, and beliefs, and then they can identify ways they are, or are not, living up to them. Developing this insight will allow each person to make positive changes to their lifestyle to align their values to those of the organization.

When the values of an individual and organization are aligned, conflicts are reduced, and diversity is embraced. The entire team becomes focused on the top priorities, and employee satisfaction and retention climbs. This alignment is a powerful catalyst, moving values off the wall and into the hearts and minds of a company and its people.

Consensus is key when dealing with a Snaker because consensus results in everyone aligning on what is accepted and what is not. The social proof model is compelling, even when we know it is being applied.

Defusing the Snaker

When I consult with companies, I typically use a combination of powerful solutions that change the focus of appropriate behavior by increasing awareness, revealing common values, and aligning people. This is accomplished by implementing a program that encourages consensus, which expands each person's leadership influence.

As we all know, one bad apple can spoil the whole bunch. Sometimes through this social proof process, a person may decide the organization's values are not aligned with theirs. If a team or corporation has reached consensus around the missions and values of the company, outliers are a noticeable "fifth wheel." In cases like this, the person very often opts out by finding another job at a different company or organization. This is actually a benefit for the company because people who are aligned accomplish more than those who are not.

Elizabeth was one such "bad apple." On the surface, she was an outstanding employee. She made her deadlines, helped others when needed, and was always polite on the outside. I did a culture assessment with the company and discovered the team was high-producing with a strong desire to accomplish goals, but they were unforgiving when a team member made a mistake and held grudges.

I began holding weekly meetings to establish a further build-out of the definitions of this company's values and to agree on appropriate ways to handle situations. People brought real issues to these meetings. I had them agree upon established definitions, and the team engaged in role-playing. The role-playing situations were formulated so the offending behaviors couldn't be linked back to specific individuals. Team members acted out both the incorrect way and the correct way to handle a number of situations.

Elizabeth, reported as the Snaker by many team members, was less than enthusiastic about participating in meetings and exercises. She spoke outwardly about how she had "actual work" to do and scheduled other things during these weekly sessions. However, her tactic failed. I had already addressed the identified cultural issues with the leader, who made the meetings mandatory.

At the outset of the consensus process, Elizabeth was visibly resistant. She made snide comments during the meetings or sat and refused to contribute. Over time, I observed that she had canned answers to things and used these responses again and again. It didn't take long for the team to notice and become bothered by it. I thought for sure she would end up being one of those people who would eventually select out of the company, which would have been a shame because she was VERY good at what she did. I knew her manager would be unhappy to see her go.

Late one night, I couldn't sleep as I mulled over how to get Elizabeth to reach consensus with her team. I decided to try three things to help bring her thoughts and behaviors to a conscience level:

1. I Powered Up by calling on Elizabeth frequently in the meetings to provide her opinion on whether the resolution to an issue aligned closely with the values of the organization.

2. Privately, I Powered Down by asking Elizabeth this simple question, "If each of our lives can be summed up with one sentence, what do you want that sentence to be for you?"

3. Then I followed up with, "How are you doing at fulfilling that description? What would others tell you about it?"

These three items bridged the gap between how her team viewed her and how she wanted to be viewed. This exercise changed Elizabeth's direction almost instantly. She quickly became the biggest support to the entire team and a steadfast supporter of the organization. Elizabeth fell right in line with the consensus of the team, and two years later, she is reportedly one of the most beloved and trusted team members in the organization.

Consensus needs to incorporate the team to be effective. Trying to deal with a Snaker alone will not produce the desired results. The persuasion principle of consensus is the most effective way to incorporate the change needed.

CHAPTER TEN

The Insulter-Offloader

Laura and her colleague had been coworkers for almost five years. Laura had been promoted several times within the department. She started out as an assistant and quickly rose to be the department manager.

She managed all the department's business and budget and had a staff of fifteen department assistants reporting to her. Although she enjoyed the challenge and mental stimulation, she often found herself frazzled by having too many balls in the air at the same time.

Late one afternoon, Laura was dealing with a last-minute work issue while preparing for her manager to leave on a business trip the next morning. She glanced at the clock and realized with a start that she had lost track of time and forgotten to send needed materials to the hotel.

She didn't take her responsibilities lightly and was distraught. The self-chastising thought, "I'm so disorganized," kept repeating in her head.

Although she understood on a logical level that she was only human and bound to make a mistake once in a while, Laura held herself up to a standard of perfection she would never expect from anyone else. To say she was already battered and bruised by her own mental perception of herself was an understatement.

Soon after this discovery, Laura's coworker walked into the office and immediately noticed the materials sitting on her desk. He was also helping to prepare the management team for the trip and asked why the documents were still at the office.

Laura explained that it was an oversight. She asked if he would be able to take the box with him on the plane since he was going with management.

Instead of offering a helping hand, her colleague responded, "No, but it's nice to know that you had a backup for your mistakes."

The words struck right at the heart of Laura's fragile self-worth. Her coworker then proceeded to hand her a presentation that needed to be completed before he left the next morning.

Devastated and deeply disappointed in herself, Laura unknowingly Powered Down and accepted the rock her coworker had thrown into her yard, even though it was not her responsibility.

Laura drove twenty miles to overnight the box of materials, which her coworker refused to take. She returned to the office, forfeiting dinner, and stayed up until one in the morning to complete her coworker's presentation.

This tactic of the Insulter-Offloader is a doozy and is one of the most frequently used in both professional and personal situations.

Hitting below the belt by eroding another's self-worth and confidence, Insulter-Offloaders strategically offend to knock us down to make us feel incredibly insecure and lesser-than. Then, when we are questioning our expertise and ability, they offer an apparent "olive branch" task or project to allow us to redeem ourselves.

And because we want to prove our worth, we agree to take on this task, a task the Insulter-Offloader doesn't want, or have the expertise, to do themselves. In a nutshell, they cut us down so we become emotional and react by giving our power away. We end up working harder and longer, doing work to prove ourselves for no additional pay, credit, or visibility while they reap all the benefits.

This may be harder to spot in a remote environment as there could be a delay between the insult and the offload of work. The need to put others down takes place when they can see or talk to another person via video conferencing or phone to have maximum impact. However, the dumping of extra work may come in the form of an email, text, or call shortly after the insult.

Identifying an Insulter-Offloader

Insulter-Offloaders are challenging to identify while in the middle of the situation. Their negative comments are meant to set a person spiraling in an agitated emotional state where logical reasoning is impaired.

It's typically easier to identify this situation after the fact. When the dust has settled, reflect on the situation. The Insulter-Offloader managed to ignite feelings of inferiority and, at the same time, have others do their bidding without a fight. They strike at the heart of boundaries and negative self-beliefs. They can offload their responsibilities precisely because they whittle away at a person's value and worth, making them feel the need for redemption.

Typically, anyone who uses insults is taking a deliberate dig at another's self-esteem. Belittling and subtly or overtly hurling insults are deliberate attempts to control others. Insulter-Offloaders are adept at sliding these jabs into the conversation so that a person may not even be aware they have been hit.

To help identify an Insulter-Offloader, do the following:

- Become attuned to notice people who consistently insult others.
- Listen for backhanded compliments designed to undermine self-esteem.
- Use the power of your intuition to notice if you're feeling under-valued and insecure around certain people.
- Be aware of people who frequently offload work to others.

Heightened awareness of these maneuvers provides a power advantage because it is almost guaranteed the person will try again. Be prepared to approach it differently next time. It is acceptable to refuse to take on a task that someone is attempting to offload.

It is also not good for our self-worth to fall prey to taunts and insults. Remember the childhood saying, "I'm rubber, you're glue, whatever you say bounces off of me and sticks to you." Take that to heart.

Each of us defines our value. Unless someone is a trusted ally or offers valid, constructive advice or insights, what someone else says should bounce right off. We should defend our worth. When an Insulter-Offloader attempts to pass off a task or project, pick up the rock that was thrown into your yard and gently toss it straight back over the fence.

Erosion of Worth

The Insulter-Offloader feeds on those who underestimate their personal power, knowledge, skills, and achievements and beat themselves up if they make a mistake.

Most people pride themselves on juggling many things and doing an exemplary job at them all. This "Superperson" complex results in individuals who overwork themselves in an attempt to prove their worth and value, but in the long run, this level of perfection and productivity is unsustainable.

Insulter-Offloaders know how to maneuver situations to their advantage by corroding others' self-esteem and feeding on a person's innate self-critical nature. They understand and exploit the "Superperson" phenomenon, knowing that most people will do whatever it takes to prove themselves and regain the trust and respect of their manager, colleagues, friends, and family members.

Negative belief systems are the fodder of Insulter-Offloaders. By eroding a person's self-esteem, Insulter-Offloaders lure others into taking on extra work and responsibility.

Many people are unsuspecting of the deliberate maneuvers of Insulter-Offloaders. Their blatant, direct, and purposeful assault on another's self-worth and competency is a stinging blow. Because most people strive to excel at their jobs—be it inside and/or outside of the home—these personal attacks are arrows that strike directly in the bullseye of self-esteem. These onslaughts leave a person reeling, the emotional wound eroding away at the value they thought they offered. The individual will then often internalize these strikes, taking ownership when there is actually nothing to prove.

The Insulter-Offloader bets that the now emotionally scorned person will gladly relinquish power, accept the proffered project or task, work long hours, and produce outstanding results in an attempt to recover. When the Insulter-Offloader says, "Jump!" the target, determined to prove their worth, will likely ask, "How high?"

This emotionally based yet very subtle strategy is found in companies, friend groups, and even families. It never benefits the one who has been insulted. Often these people regularly lose out on claiming credit for a job well done and forego the financial rewards associated with it. And to top it off, their self-worth has been riddled with belittling bullet holes, which they have accepted.

Diffusing the Insulter-Offloader

If you are the one being taken advantage of by an Insulter-Offloader, the first step is to realize there is power in knowing your worth. Someone else's insidious comments, slights, and put-downs should not be absorbed into your belief system.

The key to deflecting the Insulter-Offloader is to respond thoughtfully and intentionally instead of reacting viscerally. When they throw out their belittling bait, do not bite. Don't take the insult to heart; if necessary, vent to a trusted ally outside the office, but when in the midst of the situation, remain outwardly calm and unaffected. Becoming defensive, angry, or launching a counterattack will most definitely backfire.

Remember that even though the Insulter-Offloader is acting inappropriately and unprofessionally, this is a business interaction, not an emotional one. If attacked in this manner by a friend or family member, taking this same practiced power approach can help retain control and keep self-confidence intact.

When an Insulter-Offloader attacks and then extends an offer of a project, rephrase the situation back to them in a low, calm voice. "So, what I hear you saying is that, even though you didn't like my sales presentation, you want me to go to ABC client to present them with our company offerings?" This practice lets the Insulter-Offender know their attempted maneuver has been uncovered.

Make the Insulter-Offloader an alternate offer. "I am willing to take on that project, but to give it the attention it deserves, I will need to put XYZ project on hold or have you take it on." Or, "I would be happy to manage that sales territory, and since it entails considerably more responsibility not included in my current job requirements, I would need compensation for the extra work."

This application can often get the offending person to back down and realize you will not be easy prey. Play the part needed to get through the situation, but do not be afraid to hold your ground.

This offloading issue revolves around boundaries. When the Insulter-Offloader tosses that rock over into our yard, see it as an attempt to bust through "property lines." That stone doesn't belong in our yard; it belongs in theirs. Taking on responsibilities that don't belong to us, especially from those who are not our manager and don't have the authorization to assign projects, is a blatant disregard of boundaries.

It is a disservice to accept the rock. Not only does it reinforce our negative belief systems, but it ultimately harms the person for whom the rock/project was intended. This is never good for the personal development of a team or clients, nor does it benefit the company. Step into your power, maintain boundaries, and gently toss that stone back.

When Insulter-Offloaders Bust through Boundaries

I couldn't believe my eyes when I watched my friend Lucy's sister use an Insulter-Offloader strategy on her. Her family was gathered at a nursing home with a few close friends to spend time with Lucy's father before his imminent passing.

Douglas had a medical condition that had been overlooked by his regular doctor, and because it went untreated, it resulted in his organs failing. However, one could also say that at ninety years old, it could just be old age. As a registered nurse, Lucy felt a sense of responsibility for not catching the underlying condition and not seeking more advanced medical attention. She confessed that she felt like she had let her family down.

Lucy hadn't gotten much sleep over the past few weeks. I could see she was exhausted, hadn't taken time to care for her own needs, and was beginning to break under the pressure of the demands placed on her.

Douglas had been alert and active for a few days. Being able to spend time with him gave the family a calmness and sense of peace. I was there as moral support for Lucy and her family. I had known them for many years and considered them to be my second family.

His organs failing quickly, Douglas was not expected to make it through the night. The family gathered together to say their goodbyes and carry out his final wishes. During this solemn and heartbreaking time, I couldn't believe my eyes when I saw the smoothest Insulter-Offloader move I had ever witnessed in a family situation.

Lucy's sister, Denise, had been appointed to take care of the family's everyday financial business. As a nurse, Lucy was responsible for overseeing the healthcare needs of their parents. Unlike her siblings, Denise hadn't spent much time around the family after she left home. A "get it done quick" type of person, Denise had the attitude of not wanting to be bothered by her appointed task.

The siblings gathered around their father, holding his hands and making sure his last moments were comfortable. Denise caught Lucy's eye and, with a smile bordering on a smirk, said to her grieving sister, "Well, I guess as an RN, you sure didn't see this coming, did you?"

I watched as Lucy visibly shrunk in her chair, tears welling in her eyes as her sister's arrow struck the bullseye of her self-incrimination. Already beating herself up about her father's illness, Denise's undercutting comment had Lucy teetering on an emotional edge. Logically, she knew there wasn't much anyone could do for their ninety-year-old father; it was just his time. But even so, Denise's remarks stung, and her self-doubt began bubbling to the surface.

Lucy held back her tears and regained her composure, but it was clear she had taken the hurtful comment to heart. After a few minutes, Denise turned once again to her sister and said, "Hey, I need your help. I've been trying to get ahold of the Social Security office to change Mom and Dad's address. Every time I call, they say the wait is over two hours. I don't have time to wait on the phone. Would you call and take care of this?"

To my surprise, Lucy simply said, "Okay."

Denise handed her the phone number and walked away.

Use the Principle of Liking

Never underestimate how genuinely liking another person can play into every situation. In fact, Dr. Cialdini identifies "liking" as another one of his six Principles of Persuasion.

Using power with an Insulter-Offloader is relatively simple. This transformation requires us to look closely at ourselves and question why we allow it to happen. There is an innate desire to be liked, but when that need causes us not to hold proper boundaries, one can easily fall into an Insulter-Offloader situation.

An important point to consider is that this has nothing to do with the other person liking or not liking us. It becomes an issue of letting our guard down and giving our power away. If we know the other person likes us, then it is an issue with our boundaries or lack thereof. At that point, the necessary work is within us. I said it was simple, but that doesn't mean it is easy.

The true work begins with us looking internally and holding firm to our worth and boundaries. Once this is done in a respectful manner, it doesn't take much to diminish the power of an Insulter-Offloader.

By holding our boundaries, we, in turn, help the other person grow. And with growth comes a deepened desire to help others. It is powerful to genuinely care about the other person and truly want them to become better versions of themselves. This is how we become the instrument of change.

CHAPTER ELEVEN

The InfoHoarder

Gwen, a successful and respected businesswoman, was working to attain a very difficult degree. The process was a rigorous one. After applying and being accepted to the program, she had weeks of studying ahead. Gwen attended and passed a course that included both written and oral exams. As her final step to achieving her accreditation, she needed to give a two-day presentation. During this presentation, she would be audited by a team of professors, determining whether she would receive her degree.

For months leading up to the presentation, Gwen studied, pouring over books and data, memorizing facts, and practicing her performance. She had weekly meetings with the head professor, who offered guidance on how to improve and necessary information to add.

For two days prior to the presentation, Gwen met with her lead professors, practicing directly with them. The initial plan was to work together four or five hours each day. But those five hours turned into eight- or nine-hour days, leaving her physically and mentally drained.

During these intensive sessions, one professor kept interjecting with new information that Gwen needed to know and include when she presented to the group. None of this was in the provided materials, nor was it mentioned during their numerous weekly meetings. Gwen found herself spending hours each evening redoing her slide deck to add this new and "necessary" information.

Finally, the presentation date arrived. The attendees filed into the lecture hall and, when they were seated, Gwen began. This was her first time presenting this type of extensive material filled with detailed statistics and facts to an audience.

Throughout the day, the same professor routinely interjected to offer up even more new information. The professor would often "steal her thunder" by jumping in and offering up details to the audience that she was leading up to in her presentation. These interjections also caused her to lose her train of thought.

At the end of the first day, the professor met with Gwen to review how she'd done and give her feedback on improving for the final day's performance. It was only then that she realized she was being graded on things of which she was not aware should be included in the presentation.

The professor reviewed a myriad of specific details that were missing in her presentation. Gwen, who had studied and prepared thoroughly, knew these were facts that had never been divulged to her previously. She was also marked down because she lost her train of thought, situations that were orchestrated by the professor continually leaping in to interrupt her.

All of this was incredibly frustrating and embarrassing, especially since, instead of taking her aside, the professor reviewed her missteps in front of the attendees. Gwen recognized if she confronted the professor, odds were that she would not pass; all the time, energy, and money she'd dedicated to this degree process would be lost. She decided to intentionally Power Down, using deference to achieve her goal.

And it worked. She took the professor's advice, apologized for asking clarifying questions, and powered through. But, during this process, her intent was to uncover vital information she needed to achieve success.

During the final day of her presentation, the professor was less verbally intrusive, although there were still occasional interjections. Gwen decided to roll with it. She put aside her notes, interacted with the audience, and ultimately passed her orals and was awarded her degree.

Manipulation of Information

Sometimes we may go into a meeting or are given a project and discover—too late—that a crucial piece of information has been withheld. This might indicate the work of an InfoHoarder.

These people thrive on gaining power through the manipulation of information and orchestrating the failure of others. To do this, InfoHoarders provide a significant portion of the details needed for a task, project, or meeting but hold back instrumental pieces that guarantee mistakes are made.

Withholding necessary specifics ensures others are working in a vacuum and virtually whatever presentation, project, or task labored over will be incomplete.

InfoHoarders intentionally choreograph the blindsiding of others around them. Their mission is to make others look incompetent and uninformed to elevate themselves by being able to answer questions others can't.

Their hoarding tactic gives them a perceived authority position that often cannot be distinguished between real authority and pseudo authority on a topic or project.

Identifying an InfoHoarder

InfoHoarders tend to go undetected at the outset, but after someone has been on the receiving end of their tactics more than once, they can more easily be identified. In some instances, it may take some time to zero in on an InfoHoarder if they are exceptionally adept at this skill.

If anyone has repeatedly provided information, whether at work, among friends, or within your family, and it is later discovered that a vital piece is missing in action, odds are you're dealing with an InfoHoarder. One of the telltale signs is when that individual jumps in quickly time and again to provide those missing details.

Here are things to look for to help expose an InfoHoarder.

- Notice if you frequently find yourself not having essential details and if so, consider the originator of the information.

- Be aware if others also seem to be left hanging without key information, especially if they are dealing with the same person.
- The same individual tends to jump in quickly and offer up the missing details.
- Look for individuals who undermine and make others look incompetent.

InfoHoarders want to appear powerful. One way they accomplish this is not acknowledging the existence of others, especially in group settings. With orchestrated and exposed (usually fabricated) ineptitudes of others, they take over, filling in the blanks, saving the day, leaving the target reeling and wondering what the heck happened.

Diffusing an InfoHoarder

Once a bona fide InfoHoarder has been identified, you can reclaim power and prevent becoming a continued target.

The approach is simple: Don't take the information they give at face value. Always seek additional clarification from someone in authority or who has expert knowledge of the project or subject at hand.

InfoHoarders have developed this defense mechanism as a by-product of low self-esteem. People who are insecure rarely empower others: Information is power and by withholding key details, an InfoHoarder attempts to bolster their self-worth. Because this lack of worth originates inside that person, an InfoHoarder's internal alarm sounds when they sense a threat.

This protection mechanism creates a considerable disadvantage for those around them. To circumnavigate this situation, it is best to Power Down in the presence of an InfoHoarder. The more these individuals feel others are not a threat to them, the more they will trust.

By consciously choosing a Power Down position, one can eliminate or, at the very least, minimize themselves as a threat to an InfoHoarder's maneuvers.

By creating an environment in which each person feels secure in their position of influence, this allows everyone to be the best version of themselves, unearth more information, and hopefully fully uncover all of the pertinent data needed for everyone to be fully informed.

This process may take time to develop and refine as "you don't know what you don't know" about every unique project and situation. A person's data mining skills improve over time, and with a genuine interest in others, we can help growth happen.

If we continue to find ourselves in compromising positions where we don't have all the necessary specifics, it is important to walk the line carefully. Avoid calling out the person in question both publicly and privately as it can backfire.

For example, if you are walking into a meeting and are just then informed you are presenting, say something to the group like, "I just found out a few minutes ago I am presenting in the forum, so I will do my very best."

This statement helps maintain our power by letting others know in advance that our lack of preparation or level of detail is not a reflection of our capability.

Use the Principle of Authority

Let's again turn to our expert Dr. Robert Cialdini and his work on influence for another power tool to employ: authority, or in the case of the InfoHoarder, perceived authority.

The first step is to determine if the supposed InfoHoarder has real or perceived authority. Many times, these people pass themselves off as holding official status when, in fact, they are creating an authoritative smoke screen.

It is our responsibility to seek informed awareness of who holds actual authority, knowing that it can be faked and misleading on the surface level. We often assign authority to people based on how they dress, the car they drive, or their own projection of authority.

Dr. Cialdini stresses that it is necessary to differentiate between someone *in* authority versus someone who is *an authority*. One dictionary definition of an authority is an expert. There is a need to continue to rely on experts such as judges, doctors, lawyers, and other authorities in specific fields because, typically, they have gained their positions and certifications through superior knowledge. However, just because a person creates a perception of authority on a matter doesn't mean we should accept it at face value.

This is where the InfoHoarder gains their power. They make us believe they are *the* authority on the matter at hand when, in reality, they are attempting to place themselves in authority. Therefore, it is important for us to have a guarded approach to situations involving authority attempts that are not properly authenticated. This awareness is key to eliminate someone claiming to be an authority when they do not hold the proper credentials or expertise.

The Power of Seeking Information

To properly position an InfoHoarder, it is necessary to change the way in which we view them. Determining an InfoHoarder's actual level of authority is paramount. Chances are they are being viewed as someone in a position of authority even if they are not.

Many people falsely believe seeking additional information spotlights ignorance and incompetence, often due to their own personal belief system.

This is an intrinsically distorted perspective, especially if there is a desire to turn an InfoHoarder situation around. It is important to understand that withholding information has more to do with the InfoHoarder than it does with us.

Their hoarding compulsion stems from their lack of confidence and self-esteem. By understanding and accepting this paradigm, we can view information as a normal part of life. It permits us to step into our power and talk to others, ask questions, and undertake research to find out the additional information needed to do a thorough job or live an extraordinary life.

As a member of The John Maxwell Team, I get the opportunity to listen to John in numerous settings. John is the antithesis of an InfoHoarder and a good role model for me because I never want to be an InfoHoarder.

What I appreciate about John is that he is curious about life. He never stops asking questions. I have learned from him that a life worth living requires a genuine hunger for knowledge. Not just for work but also about life, other people, cultures, beliefs, and ideas.

Not seeking out as much information as we can takes us away from the task at hand. It derails our purpose, our mission, and our ability to be creative. Yes, it takes time to ask questions and do research, but if we fail to satisfy our curiosity through exploration and discovery, there can be misunderstandings of epic proportions.

Many people don't feel comfortable asking questions and seeking out additional information. If you find yourself in this position, I challenge you to ask yourself, "Why don't I feel that it is acceptable for me to ask questions and seek answers? What prevents me from asking questions? Is there something in my belief system that holds me back?"

Doing some introspection around our hesitancy to ask questions and seek details can be very revealing. I believe we should never be satisfied with just the information at hand. By becoming a curious person, we cultivate an acceptance of inquisitiveness and becoming empowered.

CHAPTER TWELVE

The Negatron

vy League-educated, Sally was a well-known professional in her field and highly respected for her expertise. A company that she had sent a lot of business to over the years asked her to partner with them on a contract basis to provide her insights and knowledge on a new program they were rolling out.

Sally was honored and excited to help and knew she had value to add. She had even acquired additional education about cutting-edge technology that she knew would prove beneficial to the organization. Sally knew her stuff and was prepared to share her in-depth expertise with the project team, including Mike, the COO.

At the first high-level project kick-off meeting, the team was excited and engaged. As the meeting progressed, Sally enthusiastically shared her data and was instrumental in the planning process. But every time she offered an idea or asked a question, Mike shot her down. She was peppered with condescending remarks, including, "You don't know how we do things around here," and "Sally, just sit back and watch a while before you say anything."

Surprised by this unexpected reaction, Sally decided to refrain from interjecting her ideas for the next few days of this week-long meeting. On Thursday, Mike requested she present details on her latest training to move the project forward.

Not fifteen minutes into her presentation, Mike visibly disengaged. Not long after, he got up and left the conference room without any explanation.

The next morning, Sally was summoned to the COO's office. Upon her arrival, remaining behind the desk, Mike nodded, indicating the chair where she was to sit. As she entered and took a seat, Sally observed that her chair was considerably lower, providing her with a physical power disadvantage. She sensed a power play at work.

During their meeting, when Sally attempted to explain her ideas as well as concerns about the project path, the COO interrupted with statements such as, "What makes you think you are qualified?" and "Why would we ask you to do that? You have only been here a short time. Our team has been thinking about this project for a year."

Sally was floored. Pausing to take a deep breath, she explained that she was enlisted as a consultant precisely because of her expertise and knowledge. She clarified that she had even sought additional training on her dime to enhance her value to the company and the project.

Mike then broadsided her by stating, "Sally, I don't see your passion for this project. You used to present material with great energy and excitement, and I don't see that in you anymore."

Sally attempted to mentally decipher this unexpected message. The COO hadn't stayed to hear her presentation, which was met with collective enthusiasm from the project team.

After a few more minutes of trying to gain clarification by asking questions, Sally was no further along in her understanding of the issue. Mike continued to call her expertise into question, stating that she didn't have anything to contribute to this crucial corporate project.

Until this point, Sally had considered becoming an employee for this company. After this conversation, it became apparent to her that she was going to finish out her present contract and be done. She took her expertise and knowledge to another company and went on to lead them in an award-winning project.

Sally had to option to walk away, but often, when this happens in our core workplace, the option to leave is not realistic. So, we are left with needing to change the impact of the Negatron on us.

The Negatron

Many of us know someone or maybe more than one person who is continuously a downer. They always find fault. They always have something negative to say about everything, every person, and every situation.

Negatrons are masters at backhanded compliments. You know when you've been on the receiving end of one of those when initially you think, "Wow, what a nice thing to say," but then when you think back on it, you realize you've been insulted.

I was the recipient of such a comment after a training workshop I conducted. The person, who also taught this same course, said to me, "This is a knowledgeable group of people." I nodded in agreement, and he added, "I don't think they would have understood what you were saying if they weren't such an intelligent crowd." Wow, what a blow!

Fortunately, I received a high survey result from the attendees and understood the endgame he was using with that remark. If not, I might have needed to put my self-esteem on life support!

Negatrons love to sneak in subtle jabs, striking at the heart of our inner belief system and the often-negative beliefs we hold about ourselves. Put quite simply, Negatrons make it their mission to find out what hits hardest and use it to their advantage.

Negatrons atrophy the self-confidence of others by striking at the heart of our negative belief system.

Negatrons are people who are rarely team players. They can be more of an infestation with their "better than" attitude and their cunning ability to deplete the energy and atrophy the self-confidence of those around them.

But when it comes right down to it, Negatrons are simply overcompensating for their own lack—lack of their own self-esteem, achievement, knowledge, skill, and experience or their perceived absence of it.

Their cynical quips are a tactic to deflect away from them taking a good, long look at themselves. They often can't see or acknowledge their deficiencies or areas where they would benefit from personal growth. Or they are well aware of their areas of lack, and because they personally don't want to put in the time and energy to improve, they knock others down to keep them from growing and succeeding.

Negatrons fundamentally have to compensate for their own feelings of substandard self-worth. They do this by lifting themselves up while putting others down.

Identifying a Negatron

Negatrons are pretty easy to spot. Just look for the person lobbing backhanded compliments and insults, calling out personal critiques, and generally being a contrarian. They are the "rain on the parade" or "wet blanket" that tends to drain everyone's energy right down the toilet.

Negatrons have mastered the art of deflection. They employ this redirection strategy through the use of adversarial taunts, personal digs, and unwarranted judgments.

Negatrons have fine-tuned the ability of:

- Always having something negative to say.
- Using inconspicuous backhanded compliments or blatant insults.
- Minimizing other people's credentials.
- Downplaying any achievements that should be celebrated, individually or with a team.
- Saying things like "Let me handle this client/project; it's an important one."

If you are supervising one of these individuals, Powering Up and being too firm or direct with them, especially concerning their accountability, might cause them to feel put upon and they may make accusations that you are being overly demanding.

Deflection

It is important to remember that Negatrons are trying to deflect away from themselves. It's honestly not about us, so don't buy into their injections of negativity. The saying "water off a duck's back" comes to mind with Negatrons. Just let their comments roll right off. Put on the invisible armor of power to protect your self-esteem, knowing that their self-worth is at the heart of the issue.

Be aware in advance that Negatrons will use a myriad of off-putting tactics, including subtle or blatant insults. It is best to maintain power by remaining unflustered. Take deep breaths to remain calm when having conversations with them. Ignore their button-pushing comments; don't outwardly acknowledge that their jab has hit home.

Powering Up with a Negatron, especially when using a raised voice or getting visibly upset, will backfire. This offers them ammunition, and they are sure to use it to their advantage. If we get defensive, we can be sure a Negatron will latch onto that, using it to erode our self-confidence. Getting hot under the collar, making excuses, or defending ourselves is a sign it's time to be the bigger person, retain control of our emotions, and walk away.

Negatrons want an immediate reaction, not a thoughtful response. To provide the time and space to move from reaction to response, allow yourself a moment to pause.

Tip: When providing a Negatron with information about their performance or addressing any accountability issues, always be sure to have a trusted witness present. Having another person in the meeting will help alleviate the Negatron from redirecting the issue, and even if they do, someone else will be privy to their actions.

Wonder Woman's Gold Bracelets

Don't take a Negatron personally. When those insults start flying, think about Wonder Woman and her bracelets. When the bad guys were shooting at her, Wonder Woman would hold up her wrists, deflecting shot after shot off those golden bracelets. Wonder Woman didn't take offense. She wasn't insulted or emotional. She never once took personally what was coming at her or if she should reflect it back. She didn't return fire. Her goal was to avoid harm, and her bracelets were an integral part of that successful response.

Interactions with Negatrons are instances that frequently can be rewound and replayed in our mind's eye as if we can change what has happened by thinking about it. This is another way we give our power away. If I am unable to come up with something concrete to help remedy the problem after thinking over a situation three times, I put on my Wonder Woman bracelets. I let the insults bounce off and go on about my day.

Important Relationships with Negatrons

If a Negatron is a person who we want or need to have a relationship with, then we need to approach them strategically.

My grandmother was one of those people for me. She was a doom and gloom type of person and never seemed to have anything positive to say. In her defense, she knew what it was like to have lived during the Great Depression. She and my grandfather were farmers, and in those days, they didn't have much money.

My grandmother was also a terrible cook. Not just bad, but frightful. Even her cookies, which for a kid are sweet, yummy, and magical treats, were torture to eat. My grandmother had mastered the art of destroying cookies. It wasn't until years later that I learned why her cookies were so awful. She never used the full amount of sugar because she was afraid she would not have enough.

My grandmother always felt she needed to save things because, at any minute, the world could change, and there would be another Depression. She believed that there was never enough to go around. She learned to be frugal, to stock up and save because she knew what it was like to go without.

As a child, I never saw my grandmother smile. Not once. So, it became my mission to make my grandmother smile. I was unsure how I would make it happen, but I would not stop trying until I got her mouth to turn up at the corners. It didn't even have to be a big grin; a small smile would do. After all, how hard could it be?

"Operation Smile" went on for years with no success. As my grandma entered her late eighties, even though I was still trying my hardest, my hope for that smile was beginning to fade. Not long after I had once again tried and failed on my latest mission to make her smile, I accidentally learned the principle of reciprocity. Inherent in all cultures, reciprocity holds a powerful impact.

Simply stated, it's an internal feeling or rule of wanting to repay someone in kind for what they've given or done for us.

Use the Principle of Reciprocity

Reciprocity is a socially enforced rule, otherwise no one would be the first to give. It is found in every culture and has expanded throughout existence. It can be found in everyday life, which makes it extremely powerful. If friends invite you to dinner, you are inclined to extend them an invitation for dinner at your home. When someone gives you a birthday gift, when their birthday rolls around, you will feel obliged to return the favor.

Dr. Cialdini explains reciprocity this way: "By virtue of the reciprocity rule, then, we are obligated to the future repayment of favors, gift, invitations, and the like. So typical is it for indebtedness to accompany the receipt of such things that a term like 'much obliged' has become a synonym for 'thank you,' not only in the English language but in others as well (such as with the Portuguese term 'obrigado'). The future reach of the obligation is nicely connoted in a Japanese word for thank you, 'sumimasen,' which means 'this will not end' in its literal form."

Not only is reciprocity a powerful, innate, and accepted practice, but it is also taught by parents as a social norm. In fact, society has terms for those people who make it a habit not to give back once something is done for or given to them. Names like ingrates, deadbeats, moochers, and freeloaders are labels applied to serial non-reciprocators.

Reciprocity is so ingrained in our society that it produces a natural, many times unconscious, personal yearning to give back to the other person. It is inherently human to not want to feel indebted to others. Reciprocity taps into that desire to even the score.

Minimizing Their Impact

For me, using the power of reciprocity was what turned my grandmother's frown upside down. During "Operation Smile," I had learned that if I bought her a gift, she was always grateful, but would tuck it away in a drawer and save it for a rainy day. Therefore, whatever I gave her had to be something that had an "expiration date."

I was in high school and had taken up cake decorating. It was much more than a hobby; I had a pretty successful side business going to earn extra money, something all teenagers need! So, not meaning to brag, I was pretty darn good. I made birthday cakes, wedding cakes, cupcakes, decorated cookies, and homemade candy.

My grandmother loved sweets and never let food go to waste, so I started to bring her some of my creations. Mostly they were ones that I deemed decorating flops, but they all looked grand to her. Whatever confection I gave her, she would savor each bite, extolling the texture, the artistry, and most of all, the taste. The secret was using the precise amount of sugar, which, of course, was why her cookies fell short. But I never said a word to her and let her enjoy the dessert.

Week after week, I would take goodies to my grandmother. She began to look forward to my visits and eventually started to give me the slightest of smiles when I arrived. My treats seemed to open something positive in my grandmother. Our conversations gradually became more meaningful and honest. She began sharing with me more about her life, her experiences, and her fears. Those visits where we sat together, enjoying my messed-up cake creations, allowed me to see my grandmother in a new light.

She told stories about her and our family, sharing secrets and giving me glimpses into her past. To this day, I remember when she finally gave me a full smile. I had no idea I was giving her two gifts—the food in my hand and, even more valuable, my time and attention.

I cherish those days with my grandmother sitting at her small wooden table, eating lopsided cake and creating memories.

As a teenager, I wasn't aware I was using the power of influence and that what I was doing with my grandmother had a name— reciprocity. I gave her sweet baked goods along with my time, something that meant a lot to her, and in turn, she gave me a smile. Our relationship became stronger and more meaningful, which was something she could give back to me.

The experience with my grandmother taught me that the power of thoughtfulness and a sweet gift can go a long way toward diffusing a Negatron.

Defusing the Negatron

The experience I had with my grandmother taught me that reciprocity doesn't have to be a big, grand gesture or an expensive gift. It works even on a small scale.

Many of us have had a friend or coworker stop by the local coffee shop on the way to work and pick up our favorite drink. When we asked what we owed them and they said, "Don't worry about it," we immediately wanted to find a way to repay them for their thoughtfulness. Nobody is likely to go bankrupt over a cup of coffee, but that is not the issue. Anytime we can make someone feel appreciated, it changes everything. This is a healthy ebb and flow of power dynamics.

It is not simply the rule of reciprocity that should be the driving force that leads us to give. All of us can tell when someone is trying to manipulate us. Not only is that unacceptable, but manipulation also doesn't have the spirit of reciprocity at its core. Reciprocity is about showing others that we care, that we value and appreciate them.

That is why there is a need to examine our motives and make sure we are genuinely seeking to enhance someone's life. If that is the motive, then reciprocity is an excellent way to turn a Negatron's frown upside down.

When someone gives us a thoughtful gift, most people have an innate desire to fulfill the rule of reciprocity, or we are left feeling off-balance.

When using reciprocity, it is best to start with small gifts or concessions because we are not trying to buy the person but create a different interaction energy. Gestures that are too expensive or flashy may be viewed by the recipient as a manipulative power play tactic and could backfire.

Remember, this is about igniting the reciprocity principle, not trying to make the other person indebted because that will never work. It is about building relationships that are positive and up-lifting.

Give it a try; it's fun. Surprise someone—let them know how much they are valued and appreciated.

CHAPTER THIRTEEN

The Swoop and Poop

I was getting ready for my first big presentation in an industry unfamiliar to me. I was outwardly nervous, which doesn't usually happen to me, but those close to me could tell I was anxious. My nerves sprang from the impact I knew I could have on the group, but I couldn't fluently speak their jargon. This "language gap" was shaking my confidence.

However, I had done my research and worked hard to understand this industry's struggles and challenges. I wanted to offer them the best my fledgling company had to offer, which would help them work closely with their organization's leaders.

So, although I knew little about their industry, I knew quite a lot about their obstacles in communicating with the C-suite executives. As this realization happened, my nerves gave way to excitement at being able to share my knowledge, this time from the other side of the table. I felt confident. And that's when it happened.

A friend advised me by saying, "You know, it doesn't really matter what you say to them. Wear a skirt and high heels, and you'll be a hit."

Wow, did I hear what I thought I heard? High heels and a skirt are all that mattered?

It was a hard hit. The comment took the air right out of my balloon. I felt like my parade hadn't only been rained on but pooped on.

The fact that my friend was a female engineer made the impact of her comment even more devastating. She knew the field very well, and while conducting my research and creating my slide deck, I had asked for her input numerous times. She had offered some valid points for improvement while also commenting that my work was impressive.

Now that I've had some distance from the experience, I can see how Swooping and Pooping could be developed into a finely crafted art. Whenever I was embarking on something new or had reached a major milestone, I realized that even though we hadn't communicated for weeks or months, she would often swoop in, poop a pile on me, and then be gone just as fast.

She was a close friend and should have been my biggest supporter. This accounted for why her comment affected me so profoundly. But there was more to it. I had seen this behavior time and again over various things yet couldn't understand why it took such a powerful, emotional hit on me, especially when I saw the pattern.

In this particular instance, I wanted to consciously counteract the feeling going on in the pit of my stomach. So, I Powered Up and faced it head on. First and foremost, I resolved not to let the comment get to me. I also thoroughly reviewed my presentation to ensure I was fully prepared.

My friend, a masterful Swoop and Poop, was dumbfounded the next time she made a snarky comment as to why I was not upset. Realizing she had double pooped on me, both as a woman and professionally, I reclaimed my power. This time she didn't have the same impact as her previous dive and dumps.

Once I realized what was happening, I deflected these crappy comments and vowed never to let a Swoop and Poop upset me again.

Emotional Havoc and Derailing Focus

It doesn't take long to name the person who loves to drop that pile on us. They do it by creating emotional havoc, sometimes dumping extra work as they fly on by.

Swoop and Poops are incredibly easy to spot. Often the staff will identify that such a person exists but will probably not reveal their name. As a foundation executive, it seemed there was always one board member who would pull a swoop maneuver. These individuals rarely came into the office, but I almost always had a pile to clean up after they left.

I recall one particular board member who reduced my team member, Megan, to tears after such a dive bomb.

Megan was a very detailed worker who spent considerable time and energy making sure the board minutes were thorough and properly formatted.

After one board meeting, this Swoop and Poop walked over to Megan's desk and tossed his copy of the minutes at her with an exaggerated flourish. "These are all wrong. Our board minutes should be recto verso. You've been doing this long enough that you should know this by now. Pay attention and get it right." And off he went.

Megan didn't know what that term meant but was convinced she had done it wrong and deserved the board member's harsh criticism.

I was left with the aftermath of this extremely conscientious worker now thinking she had committed a cardinal sin. The entire team was upset because Megan, who was the poster child of never getting upset or shaken no matter what occurred, was so upset by this Swoop and Poop.

I instructed another member of the team to look up the term and print out the definition. Megan had been correctly formatting the minutes, but I wanted to use this experience as a teaching moment for the team.

Soon the team member returned to share the definition. In a nutshell, Megan had missed numbering a blank page in the addendums of the board packet. But rather than politely mentioning the oversight and asking Megan to correct it, this board member chose to Swoop and Poop, causing unnecessary drama and setting the team back an entire afternoon of work over a blank page and its numbering.

The difference between the Negatron and a Swoop and Poop is distinct. The Negatron is persistent and relentlessly negative, but the Swoop and Poop swoops in quickly, poops on the parade, and leaves just as fast.

Swoop and Poops fly by, dumping comments that derail focus onto issues that are irrelevant.

The Swoop and Poop rarely misses an opportunity to question and challenge everything, but unless they are doing a fly-by to dump their off-putting comments, they tend to be elusive.

They derail focus and turn attention to items and issues other than those that matter. This can be done in person or in the form of an email or phone call. Those who've been pooped upon spend useless hours of work or worry that drains them of valuable time and energy. We get to the point of dreading their impending arrival and get anxious when they come to the office. When an email from them arrives in your inbox, you will audibly groan, and your palms may involuntarily sweat.

Again, because of their past dive and dumps, these Poops cause high levels of anxiety even when they are not physically present. Unless we are aware of their end game, we will get caught up in a cyclone of self-doubt and find ourselves catering to all of the Poop's request with high emotional energy.

Identifying a Swoop and Poop

These people are easy to spot as they leave a big wake long after leaving the building or sending that email. The way I associate Swoop and Poops is to remember the scene out of the 1990's movie *Top Gun* which, if you haven't seen it, is about navy pilots trying to make it through advanced military training.

The main character, Maverick, and his partner, Goose, do an unauthorized fly-by of the tower. It is loud, disruptive, and rattles everyone in the tower, including the officer in charge, who is so stunned he spills his coffee down the front of his uniform, letting out a few choice words in response.

Poops love to swoop in, create havoc, drama, and chaos, then off they go until their next fly-by. They have a dive and dump *modus operandi*, which is deployed every time they come on the scene. The unsettling wake they leave will be felt, seen, heard about, or experienced by all.

Identify a Swoop and Poop by watching for these things:

1. They rarely stay for an entire meeting. Poops only hang around long enough to drop their negative bomb and then they are off.

2. They do their best to avoid interactions with specific individuals.

3. Poops typically don't contribute anything significant to projects.

Diffusing the Swoop and Poop

Unlike the other identified situations, this one is the hardest to manage as it almost instantly brings high emotion. The power antidote is not external but internal and, just like the Insulter-Offloader, is wrapped up in our belief system. That's right, once again our belief system is at work.

Once someone is established as a Swoop and Poop, understand that their tendency to dump on others is not just a one-off situation or a problem they are trying to manage. The Swoop and Poop's behavior happens consistently and continuously, but not always to you.

There are three secrets to dealing with a Swoop and Poop, and they're simple but effective.

1. You can always reclaim what happened—even if you didn't respond well at the time—by realizing it was about them, not about you.
2. Prepare for it to happen.
3. Realize it won't happen very often to you.

One of the most effective ways to handle Swoop and Poops is by appropriately leading ourselves and our team (and by default the Poop) when these kinds of things happen. Yes, I said lead!

If we are waiting for a Swoop and Poop to miraculously wake up one day and realize what they are doing, we probably should be spending our days at Disneyland where dreams come true and every day can be magical. (For those who have been to Disneyland, we know that even at the most magical place on Earth, children still cry, parents lose their temper, and stress levels get high while waiting in those long lines.) As empowered professionals, we must lead and respond, not react.

Expect the behavior out of a Swoop and Poop and prepare for it. Then when we pause and respond rather than react impulsively, we can diminish their power.

Consider the Navy Seals. Part of their extreme success comes from how they study every possible situation that could go wrong on a mission. The team then prepares for and practices their response repeatedly. This same method is good preparation if we want to reclaim our power around a Swoop and Poop.

Perhaps one of the reasons Swoop and Poops have such a profound impact on us is that they swoop in unexpectedly and for such a short time. It makes it hard because these individuals are often people we want or need to maintain a good relationship with, like senior executives, volunteers, or in my case, a longtime friend.

To understand the "why" behind how much they can disturb us, let's look at the principle of influence Dr. Cialdini refers to as scarcity.

Use the Principle of Scarcity

Dr. Cialdini refers to scarcity as "The rule of the few." In this case, because a Swoop and Poop happens infrequently and in short bursts, we can be blindsided. And we're even more in a bind because we want to make sure we don't damage or lose our relationship with them.

And it's precisely because these interactions are so infrequent that we give them more emotional weight.

Anyone who is a collector understands that any item, such as baseball cards, stamps, artwork, antiques and such, holds more value when it is one of only a few rather than one of many.

The weakness we fall prey to regarding scarcity is that more value is placed on things that are infrequent and harder to obtain. A great example of this is Black Friday. Crowds of people swarm to malls and stores to get one of a "limited quantity" of an item at a special price. Because there are only a few of these items, people behave in ways they would not otherwise. Pushing, crowding, shoving, yelling… and that's before the store even opens!

There is an instinctive emotional reaction to scarcity, no matter what it is.

But in the case of dealing with a Swoop and Poop, we can actually use this to our advantage.

Let's review what we know. We know from the principle of scarcity that when things don't happen very often, we react stronger to them than we otherwise would.

When a Swoop and Poop shows up, dumps on us, and then leaves, we can recognize that this is not a "normal" everyday occurrence. It doesn't happen very often. Even if it's the same person who repeatedly Swoops and Poops, it's still not something that happens every day.

Remember the friend who made the cutting remark to me where she dissed my presentation by saying, "It doesn't really matter what you say to them. Wear a skirt and high heels, and you'll be a hit"? I was able to calm myself down when I responded to her, and I reclaimed my power by applying the three steps: I controlled how I responded, I prepared for it to happen, and I realized it wouldn't happen very often.

And with Megan, we essentially did the same thing. I brought her into my office and encouraged her personal power by reminding her it really wasn't about her to begin with, to be mentally prepared if something like this happened again, and to realize if it did happen again, it wasn't going to occur very often.

The Swoop and Poop may not even be somebody we know or interact with regularly. This person can be a family member, friend, or coworker, someone in leadership, or a volunteer, but particularly if you're a leader, make sure it is not you! Nothing diminishes the ability to lead, influence, and be empowered more than becoming known as a Swoop and Poop.

CHAPTER FOURTEEN

Power-full Language

The language of power touches everything we do on the stage of life. However, before we can talk about how to move on the stage, we must talk about the language that accompanies power.

Leaning into our influence takes awareness and energy. To activate power externally, we need an understanding of the language of power, which is a blend of verbal and nonverbal cues, views, and actions.

But before we can address spoken language, we need to address our nonverbal cues. Humans innately defer to nonverbal cues as the primary source of authentic communication.

Nonverbal cues, or unspoken communication, consist of the transmission of messages or signals through eye contact, facial expression, gestures, and posture that accompany our words. Simply put, they are the unspoken expressions or hidden messages in which things are said or presented.

Experts estimate that 90% of the message conveyed has nothing to do with what is said but rather *how* it is said. Body language, vocal tone, and inflection are the nonverbal cues others assess to gain a complete understanding of the information someone is attempting to express. Therefore, there is a need to look at and interpret the entirety of the communication interaction.

The profound truth is that Powering Up and Powering Down often works in the nonverbal arena of communication. I can't stress this enough. Becoming aware of how we communicate nonverbally is often where we have the most influence in a situation.

Listening and Connecting

Using the language of power effectively enables us to increase our connection with others.

John Maxwell teaches that connecting is *"the ability to identify with people and genuinely relate to them such that this connection increases our influence."* Simply put, the better connection we have with people, the better the results. To increase effectiveness and learn how to effectively connect with people, Powering Up or Powering Down helps build relationships and influence potential.

It was late afternoon when I heard someone enter the area just outside my office. I worked at a large hospital, but in my role as vice president, it was uncommon that I had unexpected visitors. I heard a woman speaking to my assistant, but not recognizing the voice, I went out to greet my guest. She introduced herself as Elaine and requested my time. I could tell by the tone of her voice that she was irritated.

I showed her to my office, and we sat down at my table. After offering her something to drink, I asked, "Elaine, how can I be of assistance to you this afternoon?"

Elaine was angry and very emotional. It was apparent that she was distraught and concerned that her elderly mother might not be receiving the best possible care. I assured her I would do whatever I could to address her concerns and asked her to tell me more.

Elaine unleashed a list of issues she was having at the hospital with her mother's stay. I took out paper and pen intending to list the items that I needed to address with the hospital staff. Forty-five minutes passed, Elaine continued to talk, and I had yet to write one thing down on my notepad. I realized that Elaine was not there to complain as much as she needed a friend. She was frightened, anxious, and worried. I listened to her patiently, making every attempt to connect and comfort her. As tears streamed down her face, she told me her mother was dying.

Elaine was overwhelmed with taking care of her mother, but mostly she was lost in grief. As she told me about the toll caring for her mother was taking on her, I felt there was more to the story than just frustration. I lovingly and gently probed, asking if Elaine had family who could help. She explained she was an only child and that her grown children helped at times, but they lived in different parts of the country.

My intuition told me that Elaine needed to share with a friend, so I asked, "How are you as the caregiver holding up?" I had repeatedly seen family members so caught up in the sick individual's care that they forgot to be kind to themselves. Elaine broke down in tears. I reached out to take her hand, and she leaned in for a hug.

After a few moments, Elaine pulled herself together and thanked me for asking about her. She then proceeded to tell me how much she loved our health system and that her late husband had received care in our cancer center. Through intermittent tears, she continued to reveal her whole story to me.

Elaine had been married to the father of her children for many years. I could tell she loved him deeply, and when he passed, it was terribly hard on her. However, she said that a few years after his passing, she ran into Stan, her old high school sweetheart. Stan had remained single all of those years, stating he couldn't find anyone who could hold a candle to her. They courted, and it didn't take long before he asked her to marry him. She was so excited to find love a second time.

They were wed shortly after his proposal. The wedding was held at a country club close to Elaine's home. The wedding was a beautiful expression of love, and she was surrounded by her children and grandchildren, who welcomed her new husband into the family with joy. And the best part—they were setting out to live the best life possible with the years they had left. She was happier than she had ever been since the passing of her first husband.

However, before they reached their first anniversary, Stan was diagnosed with a brain tumor. Elaine was devastated. How was she ever going to be able to say goodbye again to someone she loved so deeply?

It was winter, and Elaine didn't feel safe driving in inclement weather. She worried about how she going to be able to get Stan to his treatments. When she was making his appointments for treatment, our cancer center offered patient transportation services.

Elaine never had to worry about driving her husband to his frequent treatments. It also allowed her to be at every appointment and feel like she had staff to help her deal with this tragedy. At that moment, I realized that Elaine was not upset with the care of her mother; she was missing the connection she had when her husband passed a few months earlier. I knew just what to do.

I called our pastoral care team, and they came to meet with her. They arranged for services that would help her and her mother. If I hadn't taken the time to connect with Elaine, I would have missed a great opportunity to understand and resolve the underlying problem. I would have also missed the chance to make a meaningful connection.

Elaine returned to my office a few weeks later with a check to donate to the health system. I couldn't believe my eyes when I looked at it. She told me she wanted to buy a van to help with patient transport and fund a driver for several years.

If I had dismissed Elaine as a complainer, the hospital and its patients would have never benefited from her extraordinary generosity. I looked beyond her words, expressed my genuine concern, and chose to connect.

It is always easier to dismiss others when they are not in the same room, on the phone, or over a computer screen. I have found it takes additional discipline to give the same respect to someone remotely as it does in person. This discipline will be the distinguishing factor that separates us from the crowd.

Actively listening and genuine curiosity to understand someone else is powerful in creating connection and trust.

"Priming"—Using Positive Words

Along with listening, positive words create powerful people. They can direct emotions, helping us to step into our power.

Studies suggest that positive words and phrases improve cognition and induce more uplifting emotions in others. Guiding others to a mentally and emotionally receptive space is a subtle use of power. Many of us employ this strategy, possibly without being aware that we're using it.

Priming can help forge genuine, positive connections. Priming is the use of stimulus words or phrases to positively influence behavior or actions. Using positive, warm, and competent words when communicating with others verbally or in writing evokes a more collaborative, positive outcome.

In emails, to convey competence, be short and to the point, and use few sentences. For those wanting to set a tone of warmth, start with a friendly greeting and add in something personal, such as, "I'm looking forward to working with you on this project," etc.

Priming takes into consideration how we want the person we are communicating with to feel, think, and act. Sterile communication may seem "professional," but it builds an invisible wall between us and those we want to reach with our message.

If we want to communicate something with confidence, our verbal and nonverbal cues should align. Capability and effective influence don't stand with slumped shoulders or speak in meek, unsure voices. They have a strong, solid posture and an even assured tone of voice.

Power and Negotiation

Genuine respect is the foundation for all successful interactions and negotiations because it leads to understanding and creating win/win outcomes for all involved. It allows us to seek mutually beneficial solutions to problems we face every day.

In fact, I love this definition from Margaret Neale, *"Negotiation is about finding a solution to your counterpart's problem that makes you better off than you would have been had you not negotiated."*

Though many people wouldn't consider themselves to be good negotiators, we engage in negotiations numerous times a day. We associate the word "negotiation" with things like purchasing a new car or with someone being pushy and aggressive. However, a negotiation process is present in most of our daily interactions with others.

Parents or those who have been around children see this brokering happen naturally and at a very early age. It is amazing how a toddler or a teenager can negotiate and yet not have any idea that what they are doing is negotiating.

Questions are the beginning of this process. "Daddy, can I have a piece of candy?" "Mom, can I have the car Friday night?" "When do you think you can have that report complete for the committee?"

But one of the basic tenets to being an effective negotiator is *knowing yourself first.*

Observing power and how it gets played out within a negotiation setting can be a fascinating exercise. Many of us feel that the goal of a negotiation is to get a deal. However, the real goal is to arrive upon a *good deal* that benefits all involved. People often get so entrenched and overwhelmed by the emotional exchange of power that can occur in a negotiation that it becomes all too easy to lose sight of the desired outcome.

Power is never to be viewed as an "I win, you lose" situation. Instead, power should be used to advance the better good for all involved. Negotiating is like sitting on a seesaw, where each person must balance their needs against those of the other party. It is possible to settle and even avoid conflict and arguments without fighting by showing up in personal power.

Let's think about the highly charged negotiations that happen in a hostage situation. I don't think many would argue that the job of a hostage negotiator entails stress levels that most of us can't even imagine. They're dealing with life and death situations where emotions are highly charged.

To the untrained person, it appears that the hostage taker holds all the power. However, the negotiators are able to get hostages freed many times without casualties on either side. But to do so, they don't overtly exhibit power. Instead, they play their power low, creating a line of open communication, building trust, and ultimately establishing a connection.

Thankfully, most of us will never have to navigate a situation fraught with such danger, but I raise this point as a way of highlighting the fact that personal power is always present and at play—even in situations where we think we have none.

Often, we tend to think of negotiating only when buying a car or a house, not realizing that negotiation is a staple in our everyday activities. Every one of us negotiates daily without even realizing it with our spouse or partner, our children, our friends, and our coworkers, sometimes over the simplest of issues.

Discovering how to use our negotiation power effectively helps us avoid igniting unnecessary battles with people.

People instinctively know when another person is pushing a one-sided agenda or they are working toward a negotiation that benefits both sides. Our goal should always be to use power productively to enhance relationships and increase influence. The proper application of power will get us far, but its misuse will ultimately lead to mistrust and the erosion of relationships.

There are many powerful tools that are valuable in day-to-day negotiations, such as speech, vocal tone, posture, and behavior. Our mindset, which includes our thoughts and belief system, and the ability to control our actions and emotions, are integral to harnessing power at its highest level.

Controlling emotions plays a pivotal role in creating win/win situations.

Consider again the hostage situation. The hostage taker is in a position of heightened stress that can quickly take a turn for the worse. The job of the negotiator is to remain calm and collected so they can "dial down" the other party's emotional pinnacle and bring them to a place of rational thought.

The best way to deactivate heightened negative emotions is by making a genuine, positive interpersonal connection using active listening, tone of voice, body language, and authentic curiosity. One of the most powerful ways to establish connection is to find a mutual similarity, especially around goals or values. This can be instrumental in alleviating awkward tension between two parties. Once a more emotionally relaxed environment has been created through connection around similarity, actively listening to the other person is the next step.

CHAPTER FIFTEEN

Power-full Connections

Active listening is a technique used in counseling, training, and solving disputes that requires the listener to fully concentrate, comprehend, and respond to what is being said both verbally and nonverbally.

To engage in active listening, focus on the words being said while also acutely tuning into tone of voice and body language. This provides a more well-rounded idea of the true meaning being communicated. We've all encountered people saying one thing, but their facial expression, tone of voice, and body language convey the exact opposite.

Being aware of our emotions as well as the emotions of others gives us valuable insights. This is where we should not underestimate our intuition because it can be instrumental during active listening. When a person's verbal and nonverbal messages don't align, listen to the cues that "speak" the loudest. In most situations, body language conveys the true meaning and emotion behind the words spoken.

Active listening takes concerted effort. It involves being fully present and taking in everything being said verbally and nonverbally by the individual who is speaking. Active listening is not about being in our own head, crafting our responses or our next move. Quite the opposite. It is about putting ourselves in that person's shoes so we can see their perspective and empathize with it, even if we don't agree. This practice builds trust and allows our responses to hold more weight.

We can learn so much from intently listening to what others say. These insights and information we gain help us navigate successfully. Once we fully grasp what the other person is feeling and the true message being conveyed, we can then paraphrase back to them what we understand them to be saying. This practice ensures mutual understanding and forward movement.

When implemented properly, mirroring is another way to build rapport. Mirroring is the subtle imitation of another person's verbal and nonverbal behaviors. Often used unintentionally and unconsciously among those who are close to us, it can foster goodwill and establish connection with work colleagues.

Mirroring is all about emotional connection.

To be effective, mirroring another person must be subtle rather than blatant. Avoid copying anything unique to that person, such as an accent or a particular turn of phrase. This can backfire as the person may feel as though they are being made fun of or insulted. It is also wise to steer clear of imitating negative body language.

To successfully mirror another person's verbal behavior, consider following their pace, tone, and volume. If that person tends to lean in while talking, stands with feet apart and firmly planted, or tilts their head when listening, choosing one of these behaviors to subtly integrate mirroring can help make us seem more approachable.

By demonstrating that we are striving to genuinely understand and connect, people will begin to let their guard down, and trust begins to form.

(If you want to dive deeper into the art of mirroring and negotiation, I highly recommend Chris Voss's book *Never Split the Difference*.)

The Power of Vocal Tone

Another "tell" of emotions that either promotes our power or undermines it, is tone of voice. When voices get louder and higher, and speech becomes more rapid, you can easily sense that someone is upset or angry. Vocal tone and tempo are universal indicators of our emotional state and, unless checked, are also "contagious." When someone else is upset, it is more likely others will follow suit and dive down the rabbit hole of emotions and mirror the reactionary vocal style.

Generally, people are naturally drawn to deep voices. Lower voices are universally perceived as calm and thoughtful. When we are in our power, we breathe deeply, our voice becomes lower and has more resonance. People who are anxious or unsettled speak at a higher pitch, often thinking this helps them be heard.

The opposite is true. To increase our power, deescalate an emotionally heightened situation, and be taken more seriously, it helps to speak at the lowest end of our natural vocal register. If we are highly emotionally charged, it helps to achieve this vocal response by speaking on the exhale rather than on the inhale. It takes a little practice, but this inserts a much-needed pause and there will be a noticeable difference in our vocal tone.

Communication and negotiation are daily human interactions in our lives. To make the outcome a success, one should reframe it as a collaborative effort based on mutual respect and understanding rather than an "I win, you lose" situation.

The Power of Being Curious

When interacting with others, possessing a genuine curiosity about the other person's point of view is a tool of power. Curiosity enables us to remain in a positive frame of mind, allowing us to connect emotionally with others and encourage engagement and understanding.

Letting go of our need to be right allows us to be curious. Understanding someone else's perspective doesn't mean we have to agree with them, but it provides information on why they believe the way they do and how they came to those ideas and beliefs.

As a coach, I have discovered that asking "how" questions in a calm, neutral tone gets people to think. "Why" questions typically put people on the defensive, amplifying the "fight or flight" mindset.

Consider the difference: "Why did you do that?" versus "How did you come to that conclusion?"

Inquiring "how" helps people move from their autopilot fast brain into a thinking, problem-solving state. Otherwise, our true intention can come across to others as if we're trying to manipulate them. We need to be genuinely curious. Questions and inquiries should be authentically inquisitive and spring from a desire to understand the other person's perspective.

Curiosity Connects

I learned the power of curiosity and connection after starting a new job at a foundation. I spent my first few weeks getting to know our high-level donors, introducing myself, and building a rapport with each person that I hoped would lead to long-term relationships.

The first week in this position, I gave my assistant a list of donors and asked her to set up meetings. When she got to Walter's name, she rushed into my office, flustered and very intent.

She said, "Gail, I don't think you want to see this person."

"Of course I do," I replied firmly. "I want to meet all of our donors."

She then proceeded to tell me that Walter was a very harsh older adult who, to put it gently, was not very nice. Walter's reputation was renowned throughout our healthcare system. At every hospital event, the organizers would assign a couple of people to watch Walter, ensuring he didn't "act up."

Walter had disrupted many events. It was common for him to walk right up to the stage, taking the microphone away from whoever was speaking, with no regard for who it was, literally hijacking the program. He would spout inappropriate rhetoric, and every time, it proved exceptionally challenging to get him off the stage.

My assistant then shared that my predecessor had adamantly refused to see him. I looked again at the level of his philanthropy and said, "He gives generously. I want to meet with him."

Still trying to dissuade me, my assistant added that Walter lived over an hour away. "I'm happy to drive to see him. Please set up a meeting." With a resigned sigh, she went back to her desk to give Walter a call.

I had handled many demanding donors and was a master at establishing boundaries, but let me tell you, nothing in my previous experiences prepared me for Walter.

Walter was in his late eighties and an ex-marine who became a state trooper after the war. He had never been married.

The fated day arrived. I parked in front of his home and made my way up the walk. I knocked on his front door to pick him up for lunch.

Walter opened the door, looked at me critically, and stated, "I don't think I like you."

With a friendly smile, I replied, "Well, let's see if we can learn to like each other."

Lunch was interesting, to say the least.

Walter made several inappropriate remarks about my appearance and even had the nerve to ask if I slept my way up the ladder to land my current position.

I gently and firmly responded to each of his remarks. "Walter, that is not appropriate." After each of his improper comments and my response, we would resume our lunch.

I asked Walter to tell me about his connection with the health system and why he gave so generously. Walter avoided answering the question every time.

When I returned to my office after lunch, I asked if anyone knew why Walter donated to our health system. No one seemed to have a clue.

Fast forward two years, I still hadn't uncovered Walter's reason for giving. My curiosity was getting the best of me. I had made it a mission to become friends with Walter and uncover the story behind his philanthropy, no matter how hard it was or how long it would take. My determination was set. I sat through monthly lunches, even eating liver and onions at one event (I hate liver and onions) to connect with Walter. He was like a vault when it came to why he gave to the health system. Even after he had moved out of the area six years earlier, his philanthropic support continued to rise every year.

As odd as it may seem, this overly brash and sometimes crude gentleman had wiggled his way into my heart. I found myself calling him on holidays because I knew he had nobody with whom to share them. I invited Walter to my home for dinner and had weekly conversations with him. He was still inappropriate, mostly to see if he could get away with it, but it had become more of a joke between us. Now he would jokingly mimic me after he said something uncouth: "Walter, that is inappropriate."

One year, on his birthday, I got up early to take him to breakfast. He was an early riser, which meant I had to get up before the sunrise to make it to his home. I had been out late the evening before at a school event for my children, so getting up at 5 a.m. was extra painful. It was a chilly morning, and as I wrapped my winter coat snugly around me, I remember thinking I would much rather be in bed.

At his birthday breakfast, Walter and I sat at the table, having our usual conversation. Like I did at every meal, I asked if he would tell me about his generosity. Today, much to my surprise, his eyes started to well up, and his voice became shaky. I had never seen Walter let down his guard, so he had my undivided attention. He proceeded to tell me his life story.

"I didn't know what I was going to do when I got out of the service. I returned home and began training to become a state trooper. My mom passed away as I was going through training, and I knew finding a woman who would marry me would be a task." He grinned and said, "You know I can be difficult." I smiled back in agreement.

Walter proceeded to tell me how he was so excited for his first shift as a state trooper. Walter explained to me with a cheeky grin that he had vowed to be kind to all the people he pulled over for traffic violations. Then the tears welled up even further in his eyes. He looked down at the cup of coffee he was holding, spinning the cup in circles. I could tell he was very uncomfortable.

After a few minutes of silence, he reached into his wallet and pulled out a picture and handed it to me. It was a family. As I looked at the photo, he pointed to the mother and said in a hushed tone, "That's Kathy."

I nodded, and he proceeded to tell me that on his first night as a state trooper, he responded to a terrible car accident. Many years before, he had pulled a little five-year-old girl from the wreckage—Kathy. Walter sat her on his knee and put a bandage on her cut leg, trying his best to lessen her fears. He talked and held Kathy, all the while knowing that after tonight, she would be an orphan before the night ended.

Walter knew the hospital was too far away for her parents to get the immediate care they needed to survive. Tears streamed down his face as he told me that he had stayed in contact with Kathy, and she now lives a full and happy life on the other side of the country. He slowly realized he was emotional and quickly wiped his face and cleared his throat to regain his composure.

Then he said firmly, "That's why I give. I want healthcare to be expanded throughout the county so it's close when people need it."

When we're genuinely curious, we often discover there's more than meets the eye. The bluster may be covering a tenderness that we may have never known existed if we hadn't taken the time to stop and *really* listen.

"No matter what message you are about to deliver somewhere, whether it is holding out a hand of friendship, or making clear that you disapprove of something, is the fact that the person sitting across the table is a human being, so the goal is to always establish common ground."

– Madeleine Albright

CHAPTER SIXTEEN

Power, Fear, and Intuition

Emotions are one of the things that make us human. No other species experiences joy, compassion, gratitude, anger, surprise, sadness, and so many other complex feelings. But when we allow our emotions to take charge of our decisions and actions, especially in a business or workplace situation, emotions can lead us astray. They can cause us to react rather than thoughtfully assess and respond.

As our lives get more chaotic, our brain has even more information to process. This increase in external data results in our fast-thinking brain frantically interpreting things on the fly. One area where the resulting decision can become blurred is when our mind arrives at a determination that may not be entirely true.

This most certainly comes into play with regard to fear. We have all felt that familiar pit in our stomach when faced with a situation that makes us stressed and anxious. This physical indicator is important when it is based in truth, but our fast brain often perceives threats where there are none.

It is much easier to approach with caution and fear instead of trusting our intuition. We have created lives that are frenetic; we don't take the time to slow down and listen to our intuition.

Intuition offers sound guidance. For many, intuition is mysterious and ethereal. Yet, we've all had it, that "gut feeling" that gives us information about a person or situation almost out of the blue. Quite a few of us don't trust our intuition, unsure how to differentiate between it and fear. That's why, before we delve deeper into exploring power tools, I want to talk more about this incredible innate ability we all have of intuitive knowing.

Understanding Intuition

Intuition is our subconscious ability to evaluate our prior knowledge and experience with aspects of the present. We process the subtle signals others are giving, words and tone of voice, body language, understated clues and information, and the overall tone and "vibe" of a situation. Combined with our personal preferences, we arrive at a place where this knowing bubbles up into our conscious awareness.

Malcolm Gladwell, in his book *Blink*, says that "intuition is a gentle inkling, a fleeting answer that happens in an instant." It's focused on the here and now. It is neutral, calm, and not based on emotion. These sensations feel right even though we don't fully understand why. They are affirming and compassionate, often "seen" first before they are felt. Intuition also embodies a sense of expansiveness and leads us to a place of knowing. But because this inner wisdom is so fleeting, intuitive impressions tend to be easily ignored.

Fear is quite the opposite. Fear is highly charged and blanketed in emotion. It is heavy, anxious, and overwhelming.

There is healthy fear designed to keep us out of harm's way, but that is not the type I am talking about. It's the fear that is relentless and restrictive, pulling us backward into the past with the goal of keeping us stuck, immobile, and afraid. It weakens our perspective and our feeling of being centered and grounded.

Our inner critic often hides behind the mask of fear, trying to keep us from stepping out of our comfort zone, challenging the status quo, or rising to our full potential. Simply stated, fear is a form of self-imprisonment.

Intuition shows up on occasion, typically for important life decisions where conclusive answers aren't readily available. Fear, on the other hand, never sits on the sidelines but is always jumping up and down, yelling, "No! Don't do it! Run, run, run!"

Trust Your Gut

It takes practice to be able to tell the difference between fear and intuition. These days, many of us have pushed our inner wisdom to the wayside, dismissing it because we can't connect to it directly. We may feel we've been taught that our intuition is irrational or may offend someone. When those "gut" feelings arise, we simply don't understand what they are, where they came from, or if we should pay them any mind.

I'm here to encourage you to trust your intuition. Learn to recognize the voice of fear and realize it is attempting to disguise itself. Gently remove its mask so you are able to see it for what it is.

Recognizing the signs of our inner wisdom is a valuable tool, one that can lead to a deeper understanding of people and situations. Trusting our intuition can enable us to fully harness our ability to step into our power by providing a sense of calm knowing.

Intuition is key when it comes to knowing the proper Power Up Power Down tools to use in any given situation. When we slow down to listen and learn from our inner wisdom instead of just reacting out of fear, we can fully assess the energy of the power play in our interactions. Doing this helps us step into the appropriate power role and use the tools of Powering Up or Powering Down effectively to create beneficial outcomes.

Driving on Autopilot

In the PBS 2020 special *Hacking Your Mind*, the host shared research stating that during 95% of our day, we function on autopilot. While on autopilot, our fast-thinking mind allows reflexive, subconscious programming to take over. This programming can be neutral, such as walking, or it can be positive or negative.

This makes us perpetual victims of our internal programming, rather than accurately accessing outside sources of information.

If we think back to the example of our minds being like a personal computer, then our software system, represented by thoughts and beliefs, can cause glitches when it comes to our response to any given situation. To enable that easy autopilot mode of operation, our brains have been programmed to react in specific ways when a person or situation meets specific criteria.

For example, going back to when I was a young child, if no one in my family listened to me, I threw a tantrum. My fast brain defaulted to that autopilot "go-to" reaction for years beyond when it actually served me. So, as an adult, although I didn't scream and yell at work, the emotions that went along with a tantrum still played out inside of me internally and emotionally. Those emotions contributed to autopilot reactions where I didn't handle influence and power intentionally.

Looking back, I know I would reactively Power Up when a Power Down move would have been a better option. Odds are there are many other of these types of scenarios that cause the circuit breakers in our minds to "trip." When we get thrust into a fight or flight situation, our internal programming hijacks us emotionally. Then our autopilot reactions and responses take hold, and if we don't do anything to change it, our influence opportunity is lost.

This fast-thinking process doesn't discern between actual versus perceived threats. Only slow thinking enables us to set aside some of our fears and reframe the misinterpretation of the feelings our physiological response evokes.

Downshifting into a rational evaluation process allows a proper assessment of the situation, enabling us to see our appropriate power role and enabling us to respond in a better way.

Our fast-thinking brain conjures up stories based on unconscious, emotional, and frequently stereotypic input by ourselves or others. These narratives then get grounded in our limited beliefs, catapulting us into a fight or flight situation and causing us to Power Up or Power Down without any real thought or conscious awareness.

In our everyday lives, these unconscious thoughts and habits become ingrained in our fight or flight response; they are then frequently triggered by something we consider a threat, such as when someone we believe to be in authority addresses us or when we are presenting to an important client. Learning how to slow down and assess our autopilot responses helps us understand why we feel threatened, leading to a thoughtful response backed by conscious decisions on how to best step into our influence by applying the appropriate Power Up or Power Down strategies.

Utilizing the breath can help slow down and break the automatic fight or flight response. This calming technique helps to center us, shifting from a reflexive state to a place that gives space to analyze a situation rationally.

The Four-Second Breath

1. Breathe in slowly for four seconds.
2. Hold your breath for four seconds.
3. Breathe out slowly for four seconds.
4. Hold for four seconds.

This methodical, thoughtful technique helps to tap into our slow-thinking, rational brain, which can help identify whether a threat is real or simply an unfounded fear or snap judgment served up by our fast brain. In addition, the time and space provided by the four-second breath places us into a position of power: The calm, slow pause where no words are spoken and no emotion revealed is incredibly impactful.

"A quiet mind is able to hear intuition over fear."

– Yvan Byeajee

Repetitive and Negative Thoughts

In addition to spending 95% of each and every day on autopilot, 85% of our thoughts around any given topic are repetitive. The process goes something like this, "I wonder what my boss wants to talk to me about? Could she be wanting to go over the proposal for our new client? What specifically will she want to know? What should I say?" This is just a repetitive sequence of virtually the same question. Repeating it over and over in our mind provides no real answer to what our boss may need.

As we repeat these questions in our heads, a strange thing naturally starts to happen without our awareness. Eighty percent of those droning repetitive thoughts quickly become negative. Before we realize it, our minds have become broken records, and we're beating ourselves up for no valid reason.

Our questions regarding our manager wanting to meet with us have devolved to thoughts like, "What if I did a bad job on the proposal? I'll bet I overlooked something important. I always do things wrong."

And on it goes. Many times, without any conscious awareness, this automatic repetitive-negative process of "garbage in, garbage out" can ring all too true when it comes to our thinking. That's why we must take control over our repetitive thoughts before they become "garbage out" in our lives.

CHAPTER SEVENTEEN

Knowing When to Power Up or Power Down

We can make a deeper, lasting impact by stepping into our power instead of retreating in fear-based emotional response. What if we used the presence of fear as an invitation to prepare rather than viewing it as a sign to automatically retreat into autopilot? What if we used the presence of fear as a "thermometer" to take the temperature of what is going on? If we can determine what is happening in the moment, we can choose to slow down, evaluate, and prepare.

The 2018 movie *Avengers: Infinity War* offers a great example of a woman embracing an all-inclusive power approach. The Avengers, a group of superheroes, and their allies protect the world from threats too large for any one hero to handle. In this film, they band together to battle their latest foe, Thanos.

Black Widow, a female Avenger (remarkably played by Scarlett Johansson), is an incredibly strong warrior who is also in touch with the power of her humanity. After a brutal battle in which she kills many enemies, Black Widow sees that her fellow Avenger, the Hulk, is overcome by rage. Unless the Hulk can gain control over his anger, Bruce Banner, the human, will remain trapped.

Knowing that, in his heightened fury, Hulk could kill her instantly, Black Widow reaches out and gently touches him. She senses that her friend needs her and naturally moves from fierce warrior to gentle friend. The power of her touch and kind words calms Hulk and allows Bruce Banner to reemerge.

This distinct seamless switch could have been because of an innate female desire to nurture. Or maybe... Black Widow felt comfortable and understood that power was simply different sides of the same coin.

People intuitively sense when someone possesses power. Yet so many of us find power confusing. We often don't know when we have it or how to use it. Though all of us want to have more influence, many of us have an ambivalent relationship with the perception of power.

I, too, have struggled with the difficult task of walking the fine line of power. As a female, I didn't want to appear harsh, cold, abrasive or be viewed as overly aggressive. In order to compensate, I have often moved too far in the opposite direction. I was too friendly and accommodating, which resulted in watering down my influence. The power is being in a position to choose what card to play.

Playing the Power Cards

Let's go back to an earlier idea from the experiment I did at Stanford University using a deck of playing cards to represent power. But we'll think of them here in a slightly different way. There are the high-power cards—Aces, Kings, Queens, Jacks—and there are low numerical power cards. Both are important and have their time and place to be used.

Playing a high-power card, or Powering Up, informs or reminds others that we are standing in our power, displays our authority in a situation, and allows our voice to be heard in the proper manner. Playing a lower power card, or Powering Down, serves to disarm and engender trust to ensure that relationships are built and conflict is diminished.

Just like playing the right card at the proper time to advance your standing in a card game, using the right kind of power in the right situations and with the appropriate timing gets things accomplished and enhances relationships. To be an effective leader and person of influence means getting comfortable using power in the applicable manner, whether that is Powering Up or Powering Down. Always defaulting to the high-power card will lead to confrontation and figurative head-butting.

It is important to recognize our natural inclination when it comes to power. For those of us who feel more comfortable with Powering Up, working on refining our ability to Power Down can serve us well. There are times when it is much more effective to use influence by employing low-power responses to foster connection.

These role changes may feel slightly awkward, but they should ultimately flow from our authentic self. Responding to power with the appropriate choice will become more natural and intuitive with practice.

Both Powering Up and Powering Down are skills that can be learned with practice and implemented gradually in situations until we become fully fluent in using both sides of the coin.

The Power of Choosing

We all have a natural inclination to either Power Up or Power Down—we're not often power "neutral." To maximize our influence, we must work toward having both types of power at our disposal. The goal of *Power Up Power Down* is for you to know what power plays are available and use the most effective ones to create a better outcome and maximize your influence.

Being unaware that we have a tendency to automatically use either high-power or low-power plays means that we are not using our influence thoughtfully and productively.

To access power and employ it effectively, it is vital to shift from a habitual reaction to a thoughtful response based on the situation at hand and the players involved.

As a female executive, I've learned that Powering Up all the time usually gives women the reputation of being labeled as "difficult." Yet, defaulting to Powering Down all the time may gain us likability but often leads to little influence. Both of these stances impact the ability to collaborate effectively.

Women can be effective and influential leaders without having to Power Up in an aggressive, oppressive, or unkind manner. Nor do they have to sit back and let others dominate simply because social norms dictate. Aligning internal and external sources of power and using both with intention is the cornerstone of engaging influence.

The sweet spot is being like Black Widow, having a full grasp of our role given the plot at hand, understanding and feeling comfortable to use either side of the coin, and employing the correct type of power required.

Acting Out Our Power

By now we've seen that it's a myth that only leaders and those in the highest positions possess power. Of course, there is a power hierarchy that can't be dismissed, but it is important to understand that each one of us has the ability to influence others; it is just a matter of whether we are aware that we hold this power and what response works best in a particular situation.

Some of us tend to Power Down out of habit; we subtly give off cues that we are unsure of ourselves, our expertise, and the viewpoints we have to share. This is communicated unconsciously through body language, speech mannerisms, and other behaviors. Frequently, we have adopted these nonverbal cues as a proper and polite way to present ourselves and make those around us feel at ease. However, when we are talking about Powering Up, that never means being a bully. It is possible to Power Up and firmly make it known that we possess control while being courteous and kind.

Some people instinctively and automatically take up a lot of space. These individuals, whether they are intentional or not, are displaying power by making themselves comfortable, spreading out with their bodies, their belongings, and sometimes their voices. This practice is also found in the animal kingdom. Peacocks, bears, and other animals make themselves large by puffing out their chest, spreading wings or limbs wide, and possibly standing upright. Among animals and humans, taking up space is a very visible indicator of power.

Others might be taught through societal and cultural norms to defer power by taking up as little physical space as possible. In order to not be rude and take up space, they can be seen crossing their legs or holding their hands clasped in their laps or in front of them. They might tuck their belongings beneath their feet or in a small, tidy pile on a meeting table. All of these are physical restraints that downplay our ability to project power.

Most cultures identify space-claiming with those who have authority and power. But as experts have proven, we all can learn and have the opportunity to enhance our influence.

True power is not attempting to manipulate, intimidate, or control, but to move relationships forward, building trust, and forging collaboration and open communication.

There Is No Shortage of Power

Remember, there is more than enough power to go around (power is basically energy and unlimited), but we each need to step into the power role available to us given the situation and the players involved.

We can use power appropriately by identifying the win/win outcome to be achieved and emphasizing the context with the influence we possess in the moment.

Power used simply for power's sake—to intimidate or control others—lacks integrity, connection, and respect.

Our perception of power plays a large role in our relationship with it. By tapping into the full deck of power cards at our disposal, we can exhibit both strength and compassion.

After we have determined if we default to Powering Up or Powering Down, one of the simplest ways to broaden our power fluency is to choose two or three power plays and begin to practice them.

For example, if you lean more toward playing low-power cards, you may decide to practice Powering Up by keeping your head still, standing or sitting in a more expansive manner, and speaking in a lower, slower tone.

For individuals who need to practice playing low-power cards, taking up less space, nodding in agreement, and asking for input are all ways to begin adding this deferential power move into your vocabulary.

As the new power plays feel more natural, choose a few more and practice those. In this manner, we will expand our ability to employ most, if not all, the cards in the power deck.

As with everything, it takes time and practice to broaden our power vocabulary. We can begin today to reprogram our default tendencies.

CHAPTER EIGHTEEN

Power Tools

As I mentioned earlier, my dad loved his yard, and every weekend in the fall, he would spend hours cleaning up leaves. Our property was surrounded by many mature trees, so this undertaking was a large one and required the right tools. Initially, he used a large rake but soon discovered that a leaf blower was a better fit for the job. For years, he tended the yard, using that blower to coax the fallen leaves into piles he could easily dispose of.

One chilly afternoon, he stood surveying our property after a large storm had blown through. The yard was blanketed in a tapestry of orange, yellow, and brown leaves. He had his work cut out for him.

Firing up his trusty leaf blower, he got to work. An hour later, he had made progress, but there was still a long way to go. As he swept the blower from side to side, encouraging the stubborn, damp leaves forward, he accidentally hit the trunk of a tree with the end of the leaf blower, knocking off an attachment.

As soon as the piece fell away, a powerful burst of air shot from the end of the nozzle. The leaves lifted easily off the ground, pushed forward by the increased air flow from the blower. Dad finished tidying the yard in record time now that he had the full power of the leaf blower at his disposal.

For years, he had been using the proper tool but didn't realize that one thing was holding back his progress.

Power works the same way.

So often, we get in our own way when it comes to properly utilizing our power. And other times, we don't understand what tools to use or how to use them most effectively.

This holds true for Powering Up and Powering Down.

By its name alone, one would think Powering Up would be the best tool to access power effectively. Conversely, it would seem that Powering Down would involve relinquishing power. But both of these tools can be used to enhance or move up the power continuum if used properly.

Choosing Your Power Positioning

To determine our power role and to employ it effectively, we must assess both the situation and people involved. Try to be clear on the mutually beneficial outcome in order to determine whether our role is to Power Up or Power Down.

Many of us naturally gravitate to either Powering Up or Powering Down. The goal is to strive to adopt a blended power style, one in which we have a full deck of power cards at our disposal.

Those who feel more comfortable Powering Down would grow by focusing on mastering some high-power cards. People who tend to Power Up would grow by incorporating more low-power behaviors into their influence repertoire.

There are three simple steps that can allow us to choose our power positioning effectively:

1. **Determine** where we naturally gravitate on the power spectrum. Consider the list of low- and high-power plays and see if any sound familiar. Or ask a few trusted people—those closest to us can often provide helpful insights we may overlook.

2. **Assess your behavior.** Keep a list of the power plays and note which ones you default to and use in various situations.

3. **Experiment** with adopting new power cards into your influence vocabulary. Attempting to master them all isn't necessary. Instead, pick one verbal and one nonverbal marker and try them out. As those start to feel more natural, pick a few others.

Adopting every high or low power card isn't necessary or realistic, but having a solid understanding of verbal and nonverbal cards will enhance your influence and help build lasting relationships.

Power Up Identifiers

It is not always prudent to "fight fire with fire." Some people approach every situation with dominance. We've all seen two people "go at it" in a meeting, posturing with overbearing body language, raising their voices to get their ideas heard, and constantly interrupting. This type of interaction can quickly escalate as both people are employing high-power positions, but neither is listening to the other. There is no collaboration, true conversation, or sharing of ideas and information. It is all about who will win the battle.

Because of innate personality or social norms, many people are ingrained from childhood to unconsciously and unintentionally default to Powering Up behaviors. These Power Up moves manifest in a variety of ways:

- Slow speech
- Low tone
- Slightly louder volume but not shouting
- Use of pauses for effect
- Stand up for others
- Lots of acronym use
- More formal speech
- Abrupt topic shifts
- Declarative statements
- Use humor
- Take up lots of space
- Use large, sweeping gestures
- Arrive with only what you need
- Place elbows on chair arms or wrapping arm around back of chair
- Shoulders back
- Firmly planted feet
- Show little emotion
- Eye contact when speaking
- Lift chin and look down
- Disregard others' reactions to what you are saying
- Smile big and often
- Show confidence in what you're saying

- Comfortable using silence
- Use few words in emails and take time to reply versus responding immediately

Those individuals who most often default to high-power plays might be served well by bringing low-power moves into their power vernacular. However, Powering Up at the right time and in the proper manner can increase our ability to be heard and tip the balance of influence in our favor.

Over the years, I have learned that groups whose voices are often overlooked or have the same opinion should avoid sitting together in meetings; when sitting together, your voices come from the same space in the room and are often portrayed as "one voice." Instead, spread out intentionally so your voices come from different areas of the room, clearly stating it is more than one person's opinion.

Powering Up reminds others and ourselves that we have something grand to offer. It accelerates our influence, showing that we are in command, self-assured, and in control of ourselves.

Power Up Moves

If you want to embrace Powering Up, here are some areas of focus.

Take responsibility for decisions

Making decisions is part of influence. Owning those decisions, be they right or wrong, earns us respect from others.

Control the bobble head

The manner in which we hold our head exhibits authority. When playing high-power cards, it is essential to keep our head

still and avoid nodding or looking around. Tilting our chin up-
ward slightly and looking down is a subtle yet distinct Power Up
move.

Claim your space

An easy way to ease into Powering Up is to begin taking up
more space. Sit or stand with feet slightly apart and firmly placed
on the ground. Keep shoulders back and chest open. Spread out
papers on the conference table. Use sweeping hand gestures.

Become comfortable with attention

Some people love being in the limelight. Others shy away from
having the spotlight shown on them. People with influence must
stand in the spotlight. It is part of showing up, leading others, and
navigating to mutually beneficial solutions.

Be in control of emotions

Having control over our emotions allows us to stand in our
power. When we allow our emotions to overpower rational thinking, we have relinquished control. Learning to regulate our emotions, responding calmly rather than having knee-jerk reactions, is
a key source of accessing and imparting influence. Remember: The
person who loses control first, loses.

Be low, slow, or silent

Speaking slowly in the lowest natural register that your voice
allows commands power. Slow down or pause to emphasize a
point. Whispering is an effective way to capture the attention of
others almost immediately. Drawn out moments of silence are the
Ace in the deck of power cards.

Power Down Identifiers

Because of innate personality or social norms, many people are ingrained from childhood to unconsciously and unintentionally default to Powering Down behaviors. These Power Down moves manifest in a variety of ways:

- Rushed speech
- High tone
- Softer volume
- Frequently using "er" or "um"
- Apologize for things
- Explain what you just said
- Raise your voice (yell or shout)
- Let others interrupt you
- Overly empathetic responses
- Relaxed pronunciation
- Inclusive language (we, us, ours)
- Less humor
- Use very little physical space
- Move to give others more room
- Make yourself small—crossing legs and arms
- Extensive notetaking
- Shoulders forward
- Shift weight
- Show emotion
- Use speech qualifiers such as: I think, just, in my opinion, so, actually
- Break eye contact
- Keep your chin down
- Watch for approval of others
- Glance around/look away
- Look down

- Justify, overshare, or provide excuses for our actions or beliefs

These are just some of the Power Down moves that, if not used appropriately and with intention, relinquish our influence. These sometimes-habitual downplays of power can diffuse or negate our influence, telling others that we aren't worth taking seriously or often even acknowledging.

When we simply default to Powering Down, we are not thoughtfully assessing which power to play based on the situation and the individuals involved.

Recognizing our blind spots and power play habits is an important step in becoming more fluent in using power to its fullest.

There are instances when playing a low-power card and deferring to others enhances our influence and can make huge changes. That's because low-power plays can help create a connection with others by encouraging mutual respect. When we defer to others, listening to their ideas and asking for their advice and expertise, they, in turn, are more inclined to open up to our perceptions, knowledge, and suggestions.

When used properly, Powering Down allows us to disarm others, creating a non-threatening environment of trust just like we saw with the strong but sensitive Black Widow.

Power Down Moves

These are the areas to include for those who wish to integrate Power Down moves.

Express empathy

We must show others that we care enough to listen, to empathize, to take their advice, expertise, and concerns to heart.

Relinquish command

Allow others to speak without interrupting. Have someone else lead the conversation and encourage them to sit at the head of the table. Seek the advice of others by asking questions and listening to the answers. Take up less space physically.

Use your head

Nod to show agreement when others are speaking. Look up at others by dropping your chin slightly and looking upwards.

Allow interruptions

Allow or encourage others to interrupt you when they have an idea that needs to be shared.

Incorporate qualifiers

When speaking, use phrases such as *I think*, *it's my understanding*, and other qualifiers to downplay your power position.

Being able to use both Power Up and Power Down interchangeably as dictated by the dynamics of an interaction gives us an entire deck of cards at our disposal. This makes us better able to address situations and people with proper influence.

Using Our Personal Power

Everything begins with us realizing that we have influence and properly claiming our power. It is then and only then that we can move that power outside of ourselves to empower others.

To guide stepping into our personal power, consider the following:

- The law of power: The only one we can truly control or change is ourselves.

- Assess the cues and social hierarchy in every situation before choosing a power position.
- Always strive to be the master of our emotions. Respond instead of react.
- Use tone of voice, body movements, and speech to Power Up or Power Down to create a win/win situation by neutralizing power plays.
- Speak in low, deep tones; focus on speaking on the exhale.
- Treat others with respect and kindness.
- Approach power with intuition, not fear.
- Establish boundaries ahead of time and stick to them.
- Harness negative self-talk and replace it with positive affirmations.
- Bring habits into the conscious mind in order to effectively change the bad ones.
- Realize we work out of our fast brain most of the time. Slow yourself down to truly process all the information.
- Identify the six outlined types of personalities and have a plan to influence the situation through your response.
- Genuinely care (and hopefully like) the other person. Find a similarity and work from there.
- Know exactly what you want the outcome to look like.
- Be clear and concise.
- Reframe things in a positive manner.
- Praise others, especially behind their back whenever possible.
- Study Dr. Cialdini's Principles of Persuasion of reciprocity, liking, scarcity, consistency, authority, and consensus to utilize power effectively (I have more information available at GailRudolph.com).

- Negotiation is a part of everyday life. Approach it enthusiastically by desiring a mutual beneficial resolution.
- Have fun being genuinely curious about other people, their views, and ideas.

Having true influence and leadership is knowing how to use power properly; to empower ourselves is the catalyst to empower others. We are not in competition with each other. Our arms should be outstretched, one reaching up so those before us can guide and teach us, and our other hand extending down so we can elevate others.

When one of us makes strides and gains success and achievement, everyone benefits.

CHAPTER NINETEEN

Power-full Alternatives

Benjamin Disraeli and William Gladstone were fierce political rivals competing for the office of British Prime Minister in the late 1800s.

Winston Churchill's mother, Lady Jennie Jerome Churchill, dined with England's two premier leaders separately not long before the election was to take place.

Later she was asked by a journalist for her impression of the two men. Lady Churchill responded, "When I left the dining room after sitting next to Gladstone, I thought he was the cleverest man in England. But when I sat next to Disraeli, I left feeling that I was the cleverest woman."

Benjamin Disraeli spent the evening asking Churchill's mother questions about herself and listening intently to her responses.

William Gladstone, on the other hand, though brilliant and witty in his own right, spent the evening telling Lady Jennie Churchill all about himself.

While Gladstone wanted to regale others with his knowledge and successes, Disraeli was genuinely interested in others. His focus was on making a genuine connection and finding common ground.

Benjamin Disraeli had mastered the art of making other people feel respected, listened to, and as a result, he also made them feel important. This trait served him well, gaining him the backing of Queen Victoria, who liked and supported him even though many of her closest advisors suggested otherwise.

William Gladstone and Benjamin Disraeli both possessed power and influence, but Disraeli understood how to use his influence far more effectively. Rather than showcasing his brilliance and skills, he chose to be interested in others and listened to what they had to say.

Disraeli's Power Down move allowed him to gain the respect and support of other people and led to him becoming the next British Prime Minister.

Knowing which power to play in any given interaction is at the core of influence. Often, playing low (Powering Down) can enhance power, allowing that dominant personality to take us seriously.

Choosing to Become Power-full

Learning to trust our intuition instead of being a hostage to fear allows us to remain in control. Unfortunately, some people feel that power is something to shy away from or fear. When we act out of fear, our emotions hijack our ability to be rational and objective.

As I have said, one of the things that often keeps us in a place of fear is our limiting self-beliefs. Beliefs are our thoughts about who we are and what we can become. They are the foundation for our success or stagnation.

Whether self-talk is positive and empowering or negative and defeating, it determines our destiny.

True personal empowerment is taking control of our thoughts and limiting self-beliefs, changing them from negative to positive. This vital internal language provides the first solid steppingstone toward fully utilizing our power and influence.

As author Marianne Williamson says in her book *A Return to Love,*

"Our deepest fear is not that we are inadequate. Our deepest fear is that we are powerful beyond measure. It is our light, not our darkness, that most frightens us. We ask ourselves, 'Who am I to be brilliant, gorgeous, talented, and fabulous?' Actually, who are you not to be?... Your playing small doesn't serve the world. There is nothing enlightened about shrinking so that other people will not feel insecure around you. We are all meant to shine... As we are liberated from our own fear, our presence automatically liberates others."

The Power of Disarming

When we are able to let go of our ingrained defensiveness that so often drives our behavior and fuels our reactions, we are then able to release the chokehold we have on needing to protect ourselves at all costs. This can help us embrace the various power roles we will be called upon to fill.

Showing grace and decorum is a true sign of power. Those with a firm grasp of how to properly use power understand that disarming rather than inflaming situations shows strength, resilience, and humility.

Disarming people rather than always taking the Power Up position with others is invariably a better place to start to develop genuine relationships. When we feel the need to defend ourselves, many people automatically (and dramatically) up their power. Instead of coming to a place of mutual understanding, this power play often leads to heightened emotions, arguments, and conflict.

The Ultimate Power: Forgiveness

Many times, people do things, either intentionally or not, that hurt us. We have no control over whether or not that person ever extends an apology or shows remorse. What we can control is our ability to forgive.

Holding a grudge, plotting revenge, or harboring hate doesn't make us strong. Holding onto hate or being a victim is like holding a hot coal in our hand and waiting for another person to get burned—they don't get hurt; we do.

There is incredible personal power in forgiveness. Forgiving someone doesn't absolve the wrongdoer. But it does allow us to heal and move on. Forgiveness sets us free. It lifts the weight of being wronged off our shoulders and offers us a sense of peace.

On the flip side of this, when we have knowingly done something to wrong someone else, we should extend them an apology, and in some cases, even ask for forgiveness.

This doesn't mean apologizing for the stance we may have taken, for who we are as a person, or that we are giving in to the other person.

But there will always be instances in life when we should be sorry about something we've said or done. The act of genuinely apologizing can be a powerful component to neutralize an interaction that may have gone awry. Apologizing shows respect for another person's feelings, a willingness to communicate openly, and that we own our words and actions.

When extending an apology, it is essential to closely examine our self-talk to ensure that voice in our head is speaking in a manner that gives us power instead of diminishing it. When extending an apology or asking forgiveness, it's important that our vocal tone and body language convey sincerity to ensure our words land appropriately.

Some external responses I like to keep memorized are:

- I didn't mean to upset you.
- Wow, I'm really sorry you feel that way.
- I can see you're angry and feel strongly about this.
- I don't want to argue. Can we focus on a mutual solution?
- I respect how you feel.
- Would you please forgive me?

To keep my internal self-talk positive, I repeat the following to myself:

- My opinion and views are necessary for the best outcome.
- I am a person of value.
- I believe in myself.
- As a female leader, I naturally bring a "beneficial to all" approach.
- This is not a personal attack against me.
- Powering the wrong way will not get me the outcome I desire.
- I only have power over myself.
- Forgiveness is powerful for me, even if they don't agree or understand.

Power Comes in All Shapes and Sizes

The late Supreme Court Justice Ruth Bader Ginsburg was a perfect example of embracing and using power to make her voice heard without anger, resentment, or force. She showed up with silent power.

Soft-spoken and small in stature, Justice Ginsburg was powerful and had a huge impact. Her quiet demeanor and diminutive size belied her subversive power. She was brilliant, and despite the social norms of the day, remained steadfastly unapologetic for her intellect, drive, purpose, and self-power.

She lived her beliefs and was strategic in her work and life and can be seen using many of the Power Up Power Down tools identified in this book.

Justice Ginsburg was polite and cultured, choosing to use facts and pointed guidance to drive her position home rather than annoyance or anger. She would Power Up by asking questions, interrupting, and speaking slowly; she was masterful at using the pause to hold power.

An unstoppable force, Justice Ginsburg found ways to achieve progress one small step at a time. And when she felt advancement or equity was in jeopardy, she would speak up, saying those two words, "I dissent." She always responded by standing firm in her power. Even when she vehemently disagreed with someone else, she showed respect to whomever she was interacting.

Ruth Bader Ginsburg understood her interpersonal power and knew how to harness it. She implemented the principles and tools outlined in this book and in doing so, played her power perfectly on the stage of life.

CHAPTER TWENTY

Stepping into Power

There I was. All dressed up with everything in place, walking out of the green room about to go on stage. I looked at my watch. The event was running late. I used that as an opportunity to grab some last gulps of water. Then someone said to me, "two minutes until you're on."

I always get a little nervous when I am speaking in front of a large group, and this International Women's Conference was no different. I took a few last deep breaths as my introduction video began.

Then it hit me. The little girl who use to throw temper tantrums to be heard had found a new place on the power continuum. I was the kickoff keynote speaker addressing female power issues in the workplace.

I'd worked on this issue for so long in my life, and I would get discouraged at times, feeling as if I hadn't made significant progress. However, I kept plugging along, knowing that stepping into my power wasn't a one-time event—it was the daily awareness of choices I could make to shift the power energy that was happening.

At that moment, right before walking on stage, I realized I had stepped into my power. Not because it was a stage but because I was a more confident "me" and that I knew I was making more informed, and better, choices for myself and those around me.

This is how it will be for you when you step into your power. You will work and stretch yourself, then one day, you'll wake up and realize you made a huge leap, and you're not quite sure how it happened.

The key is to continue to step into power in the moment. Some days you'll do great and other days you will fall short. It's about exercising that "awareness and choice" muscle so your reactions become responses, and your responses become powerful opportunities.

In my experience, making a conscience choice to be empowered will open up new horizons you never dreamed were possible.

Here are some guidelines when thinking about stepping into your power (and I think the first one is key!):

- Harness the ability to laugh at your mistakes—I give myself new material to laugh at every day!
- Your mistakes are only there to help you learn.
- Embracing your power is a process, not a destination.
- Don't fall into the trap of comparing yourself to others. You are unique, and your journey with power will also be.
- We can only do our best.

- Never substitute fiction for facts when you look at your journey.
- Don't wait until you need to maximize your influence to try to learn the power tools; they take practice.
- Don't only use power just when you think you need to; become a power-full individual in every aspect of your life.

Stand Up; Don't Stand By

When my children were in elementary school, there was a big push around teaching children to be Upstanders instead of Bystanders. The equivalent of, "If you see something, say (or do) something." This is a vital piece of social education to instill in these young minds, but even as adults, so many of us still fall prey to being a bystander.

Psychologists Bibb Latané and John Darley conducted research around what is called the bystander effect. Their study enlisted the help of an actor who was placed in a situation where they appeared to be distressed and required help from an outsider. When the test subjects were alone, they were much more willing to offer assistance. But when in a crowd of people who were also actors and told to withhold aid and just "stand by," the individual test subjects were considerably less inclined to help the distressed individual.

This bystander phenomenon has been proven time and again and is a built-in part of our programmed psychology. When in a group setting, we look to others for how to behave and how to act. If the group fails to act, the bystander effect occurs. This illustrates the potency of social proof as researched and outlined by Dr. Cialdini.

One valuable and mature (and sometimes scary) way to exhibit power is to be an upstander. Being the person to come to the aid of another, even if it means putting ourselves at risk socially or professionally, is incredibly commanding.

Being an upstander can be as simple as being in a meeting, and if a colleague is interrupted, calmly stating, "I am interested in what Lucy has to say. Let's allow her to finish." If someone says something inappropriate, remain calm and use pointed eye contact. This effectively "puts them on notice." If you need clarification, ask in a neutral voice, "What did you mean by that?"

When we use power for the good of the community and to stand up for others, we forge trust and allow others to step into their power. Being an upstander can ignite a shift, creating a space that encourages others to take positive action for the good of all involved.

Assessing a situation and the people involved allows us to take the appropriate power position. Every person and interaction are different, which is why we need to have as many tools at our disposal as possible. True empowerment comes from healthy internal self-work and external, intentional use of power.

It is important to remember that attempting to assume a power role that we don't possess in a given situation can backfire. None of us holds a high-power position at all times and stepping into such a role when the power hierarchy is clearly defined not only makes us look foolish, but it retracts from the power we do hold.

Identifying the power role available should never be about elevating our own agenda or status. It should be done to promote the greater good of the company, organization, or group.

Focusing on the situation and the greater good offers helpful clues with regard to power roles. When we allow our status, our agenda, and our emotions to overshadow the situation, we can fall victim to overstepping the bounds of power available to us.

Being Aware of Power Dynamics

Not too long ago, my son, Andrew, who was living with me while looking for an apartment, came home from work after a long, hard day. He sat down and asked if I would tell him more about how power plays work. I told him a few things to be aware of and then he said something every mother longs to hear, "Mom, could you give me some advice?"

Andrew is over six feet tall and large in stature and has worked since he was a teenager in sales team positions. He's always been a "natural" and enjoyed his job. Andrew shared with me that he had been working with a new colleague and, from his standpoint, believed the relationship between them was a solid one. In fact, Andrew viewed her as a mentor from whom he had a lot to learn. But over several weeks, Andrew noticed that his co-worker had started to get very defensive around him. If he asked her a question, she would sometimes respond harshly to him.

In mulling over the situation, the only thing he could think of that could be the cause of this defensiveness was the difference in their physical size. She was significantly shorter and much smaller than him. Because Andrew had often heard me talking about power in the workplace at home, he knew there could be external circumstances, such as his height, that might make her feel uncomfortable. Valuing the relationship, Andrew wanted to make sure he understood how the power play worked and the ingredients necessary to ensure this work association was successful.

Working on a sales floor, Andrew and his colleagues are typically unable to sit, which meant he towered over this team member by over a foot while standing. Knowing his height was not something that could be changed, he asked me if there was anything he could do to help make his coworker more at ease and decrease power plays in their interactions.

I gave him some articles to read about appropriate ways to Power Up or Power Down. After giving it some thought, Andrew applied several of the Power Down ideas to put her more at ease. If they needed to talk about a work issue, he made sure to do it during a break where they could sit at the table in the break room. He was conscious of his hands and kept them more "quiet" when they were talking. He even made a point to let her know how valuable her expertise was to him.

I am happy to report that it only took about a week for their relationship to turn around, and it has continued to be positive. She is now one of his valued mentors and one of his most ardent cheerleaders.

Andrew intentionally Powered Down to create a neutral, less threatening power position with his coworker. His size and stature naturally gave him a Power Up position, even if that wasn't his intent. By becoming aware of situations and our environment, we can effectively use power to intentionally create a neutral power position. I couldn't have been more proud of my son in how he chose to use his power.

"Powering down camouflages our power, focusing instead on establishing connections, and showing respect. Powering down is non-threatening and disarming. It shows deference and establishes trust."

– Deborah Gruenfeld

CHAPTER TWENTY-ONE

The Power of Perspective

When I was young, I loved to do puzzles. It was a great way to pass the long Midwest winters. When the pandemic hit, like much of the world, I decided to do a puzzle.

It had been years since I worked on a puzzle, and I was really looking forward to the creative challenge. Excited, I cleared off my dining table and arranged the pieces by color and design.

Initially, it was easy. I found all of the edge pieces and had the frame of the puzzle put together in no time. But as I went along and the puzzle started to come together, there was one puzzle piece that I just couldn't find. I searched all of the remaining pieces, methodically trying the ones I thought should fit. None of them did.

I looked at the box over and over again. I looked at the puzzle. I walked away, came back, and tried again. After a couple of days searching for this one elusive piece, I was sure it had to be missing. It didn't make any sense. Maybe it fell on the floor and the dog got it. Or I'll bet it had been left out of the box altogether. That had to be it.

Undeterred, I kept working on the puzzle, certain that when I finished, there would remain a hole where that one puzzle piece was meant to go.

Days later, I finished the puzzle and guess what? I found the piece I was so sure had disappeared. It had been right there all along—I just couldn't see it at the time. But there it was, and it fit perfectly into my puzzle. That mess of puzzle pieces had now transformed into a beautiful picture.

So many times, our life feels like a puzzle. We wonder: Why did this happen? This can't be right. It must be a mistake that I have to go through this. But all too often, we don't have the full picture and can't see where the pieces fit.

However, just like a piece in a puzzle, what we have gone through or are now going through is all part of the bigger picture.

Without my initial lack of understanding around power, this book would not exist. I would have never been able to share what I have learned and be a better person because of it. What I thought was so unfair and uncomfortable at the time helped me achieve all I have today.

Just like putting together a puzzle, my relationship with power has evolved throughout the years.

I think it's true for all of us that if we could all go back in time, there are many things we would handle differently. But the one situation for me that stands out the most is when I was told by the

Executive Director, "You don't need a raise. You get child support for the kids, don't you?"

Knowing what I now know, I would have loved to have responded using *appropriate* power instead of reacting emotionally.

I know that using appropriate power requires effort and preparation, and I would have been ready. In this case, I would have prepared for the meeting beforehand with a detailed list of my accomplishments.

When he stated that demeaning comment, instead of a "I can't believe you just said that—deer in the headlights" look, I would have started by giving him a pointed neutral stare.

I would have look him directly in the eye and stated in a low tone, "This is a comprehensive list of my accomplishments. I am more than happy to provide you with more details and exactly how they have positively impacted the foundation's bottom line."

Then, after a strategic pause, I would have handed him a copy of my accomplishments on paper.

Would this have changed the outcome? Maybe, maybe not.

But I truly believe that if I were to handle the same situation now, with what I've learned, the outcome would likely have been very different.

I also realize that change takes time, including learning and practicing the appropriate use of power.

It was never "him versus me." It was about my having the tools to help him see clearly that I had value, and his remarks about child support had no bearing on the fact that I did a good job and was overdue for a raise.

Rather than becoming annoyed or angry, I would have employed powerful body language by taking up space at the table we were sitting at, strategically interrupted him (not to be rude but in a way to balance the conversation), looked him in the eye while speaking with a slow, low tone of voice, and become masterful at using the pause to hold power as I asked pointed questions.

Remaining steadfastly unapologetic for my intellect, drive, and purpose and holding firm in my power by responding appropriately would better serve me through achieving a change in his attitude about my work. His viewing me as a valuable asset to the organization was so much more than just obtaining a raise.

Would I have needed to resign anyway? Perhaps. But I would have left on different terms and with a different attitude and demeanor.

And for me, that would have allowed me to reclaim my power and make the situation a win/win.

As I talked about in the beginning, the subject of power is enormous. This is just the tip of the iceberg, but I hope it has given you a sense of encouragement and hope for how you can use your power and energy. You can have agency—the capacity to act independently and to make your own free choices—and be empowered in your own life.

My journey with power has been a real-life roller coaster ride. Everything I've gone through has led me to understand that using our power with awareness and intention can enhance experiences, relationships, and life in ways I had never imagined.

I've come a long way from that little girl who exerted her power by yelling and throwing tantrums. Now, I use my understanding of influence and power in all my environments—even with my siblings. We have never gotten along better than we do right now.

My siblings now know that Powering Up and Powering Down was the only thing that changed in my interactions with them. I showed up with silent power. I no longer had to argue, yell, and fight to be heard.

It took knowing how to step into my power correctly.

Remember the law of power: We only have the ability to change ourselves; we have no control over others. However, by changing ourselves, we can change the way people view us, interact with us, and as a result, change the experience.

Even if the other party doesn't know it, they are better off when we respond out of intention and not reaction—that's what ultimately creates the win/win. By not having "winners and losers" in our minds, we shift the dynamic, even in challenging circumstances.

I go back to the words of Viktor Frankl as they bear repeating, "Between stimulus and response there is a space. In that space is our power to choose our response. In our response lies our growth and our freedom."

It is my hope and prayer that you will explore your power and in doing so, you will allow yourselves and others to have a voice, be heard, and cultivate trust in relationships. When you are able to stand in your power, others are given the ability to do the same.

Power Up Attributes

—————— Conversation Style ——————

- Use full sentences
- Slow down speech
- Low tone
- Slightly louder volume but not shouting
- Use pauses for effect
- Speak cryptically with no explanation
- Lots of acronym use
- More formal speech
- Abrupt topic shifts
- More direct
- Declarative statements
- Exclusive language (I, me, my)
- Careful pronunciation
- Use few words in email and take time to reply vs. responding immediately
- Standing up for others who get interrupted
- Use humor

—————— Posture ——————

- Soft to no sound shoes
- Take up lots of space
- Spread body for comfort
- Lean back in chair
- Encroach on others' space
- Use large sweeping gestures
- Come with only what you need
- Place elbows on chair arms or wrap arm around back of chair next to you
- Glide as you move
- Little to no notetaking
- Physical distance
- Talking while moving away
- Shoulders back
- Firmly planted on feet
- Sitting in a power position to the immediate right or left of the key players
- Arrive early to claim your space

—————— Face ——————

- Controlled expressions
- Hold head high
- Maintain still head
- Make eye contact
- Lift chin and look down
- Disregard others' reactions to what you are saying
- Smile big and often
- Show confidence in what you are saying

Power Down Attributes

——— Conversation Style ———

- Rushed speech
- High tone
- Softer volume
- Use incomplete sentences
- Apologize for things
- Explain what you just said
- Let others interrupt you
- Informal speech
- Gradual topic shifts
- More indirect
- Fill silence
- Use everyday words instead of trade jargon
- Deflect praise or compliments
- Relaxed pronunciation
- Inclusive language (we, us, ours)
- Less humor
- Use speech qualifiers such as: I think, just, so, actually, in my opinion

——— Posture ———

- Choppy movements
- Loud heels—they hear you coming
- Touch your hair or face
- Fidget
- Placing yourself in a physically lower position than others
- Lean forward
- Point toes in
- Use very little space
- Move to give others more room
- Make yourself small— cross legs and arms
- Excessive notetaking if you are not the minutes keeper
- Shoulders forward
- Shift weight back and forth
- Over-express excitement
- Appear stressed or hurried
- Sit while others are standing

——— Face ———

- Show emotions and reactions
- Cover face with hands
- Cover bottom lip when smiling
- Chin down
- Watch for approval of others
- Avoid eye contact
- Look down
- Lots of head movements

ACKNOWLEDGMENTS

Thank you to everyone for encouraging me to write this book, even in the middle of a huge life-changing year for me. You taught me to really believe in myself, and that was the best gift I will ever receive. All of you have encouraged me and spoken words of affirmations that have led to the completion of this book. Kudos for pushing me to go after my dreams.

Kristen Frank, I will never forget the long hours you have helped by assisting with research, ideas for improvement, and sometimes even been my counselor throughout this past year. This book would not exist without your support and assistance.

Karen Anderson (StrategicBookCoach.com), even after late nights and long days, your guidance, direction, insights, and coaching are spread throughout this book. I couldn't think of anyone better to write the Foreword. Thank you for your patience as you coached me into making this book a reality.

Jason Clement, you have made the workplace situations come to life with your brilliant ability to capture their essence and put them into graphic illustration. Your creative ability makes me smile every time I see your work.

Sissi Haner, your amazing ability to look at details, editing, and formatting in every aspect of this book is completely amazing. You have a true gift and have been a blessing to me.

Morgan James Publishing, David Hancock, and the entire team, thank you for believing in me and taking a chance on this book. Knowing that you had faith in me helped me push on through many long hours.

My mentors and teachers along the way who have had a huge impact on my life—John Maxwell, Dr. Robert Cialdini, Dr. Gregory Neidert, Dr. Henry Cloud, and the professors and staff at the Stanford Graduate School of Business—your teaching helped me get to this place where I could put my ideas into writing. You have enhanced my life in more ways than you know.

My friends—Dr. Linda Dew, Josh Pies, Lynn Bios, Ellen Haas, Paula Uccelli, Marilyn Territo, Dawn Yoder, Marissa Nehlsen, Rick Morris, Tim Enochs, Brian Coleman, and Melinda Carver—none of you laughed or rolled your eyes when I said I was going to write this book, but instead said: "I believe in you."

My late parents, Dean and Verna Bauersachs, and Edwin Mayer (stepfather), I'm so grateful for the many life lessons you taught me as well as the value of hard work.

My family—Josephine Wilson and Andrew Wilson, my children, and Gina Bauersachs-Miller, my sister—your reassurance, support, calls, texts, ability to talk me off the ledge when things got tough, and your unwavering faith in me has made this book a reality. Thank you for helping me believe in myself and for assisting in making my dreams come true.

My readers—This book is for you. Power is a part of life, and we all have issues around power. My hope is that with insights and strategies, we can use our God-given power to help ourselves and each other. Thank you for going on this journey with me.

REFERENCES

Andie & Al. "The Goldilocks Dilemma: Why Career Advancement Is So Much Harder for Women than Men and What Women Can Do to Change That." Andie & Al, July 2, 2020. https://andieandal.com/goldilocks-dilemma/.

Cherry, Kendra. "The Fight-or-Flight Response Prepares Your Body to Take Action." Verywell Mind, August 18, 2019. https://www.verywellmind.com/what-is-the-fight-or-flight-response-2795194.

Cialdini PhD, Dr. Robert B. *Influence: The Psychology of Persuasion*. HarperCollins, 2009.

Cloud, Henry, and John Sims Townsend. *Boundaries: When to Say Yes, How to Say No to Take Control of Your Life*. Grand Rapids, MI: Zondervan, 1992.

"The Codfish/Catfish (Short Story)." Psyche-Life, January 6, 2013. http://psyche-life.blogspot.com/2013/01/enemies-short-story.html.

Connick, Wendy. "What Is Mirroring?" The Balance Careers, September 17, 2020. https://www.thebalancecareers.com/what-is-mirroring-2917376.

"Does the Squeakiest Wheel Get the Most Grease?" *Harvard Business Review*, Sep/Oct 2019.

Duncan, Rodger Dean. "Are You A Creative Or Reactive Leader? It Matters." *Forbes* Magazine, February 13, 2019. https://www.forbes.com/sites/rodgerdeanduncan/2019/02/13/are-you-a-creative-or-reactive-leader-it-matters/

Edwards, Vanessa Van. *Captivate: The Science of Succeeding with People.* UK: Portfolio Penguin, 2018.

Gates, Melinda. "Gender Equality Is Within Our Reach." *Harvard Business Review*, September 26, 2019. https://hbr.org/2019/09/gender-equality-is-within-our-reach.

Gates, Melinda. *The Moment of Lift: How Empowering Women Changes the World.* Flatiron Books, 2019.

Gladwell, Malcolm. *Blink: the Power of Thinking without Thinking.* New York: Back Bay Books, 2007.

Gruenfeld, Deborah. *Acting With Power: Why We Are More Powerful Than We Believe.* Currency, 2020.

"Hacking Your Mind: Living on Autopilot." PBS SoCal. Oregon Public Broadcasting, September 9, 2020. https://www.pbssocal.org/programs/hacking-your-mind/living-on-auto-pilot-5p5jct/.

Kabir, Homaira. "Going with Your Gut: How to Tell the Difference Between Fear and Intuition." Happify Daily. Accessed January 20, 2021. https://www.happify.com/hd/tell-the-difference-between-fear-and-intuition/.

Kahneman, Daniel. *Thinking, Fast and Slow.* New York: Farrar, Straus and Giroux, 2001.

Maxwell, John C. *Developing The Leader Within You 2.0.* HarperCollins Leadership, 2019.

Millett, Maria. "Challenge Your Negative Thoughts." Michigan State University Extension. Stress Less with Mindfulness, March 13, 2017. https://www.canr.msu.edu/news/challenge_your_negative_thoughts.

Neale, Margaret Ann, and Thomas Lys. *Getting (More Of) What You Want: How the Secrets of Economics & Psychology Can Help You Negotiate Anything in Business & Life.* London: Profile Books, 2016.

"The North Wind and the Sun." Library of Congress, *Aesop's Fables.* http://read.gov/aesop/143.html.

Pate, Deanna (Lazzaroni). "The Top Skills In Demand For 2020—And How to Learn Them." LinkedIn Learning Blog, January 13, 2020. https://www.linkedin.com/business/learning/blog/top-skills-and-courses/the-skills-companies-need-most-in-2020and-how-to-learn-them.

Peterson, Suzanne J., Robin Abramson, and R.K. Stutman. "How to Develop Your Leadership Style." *Harvard Business Review,* Nov/Dec 2020.

Puiman, Rosalie. "Your Gut Feeling: Fear or Intuition." HuffPost, December 6, 2017. https://www.huffpost.com/entry/your-gut-feeling-fear-or-_b_6667194.

Rudolph, Gail D. "Using Science & Knowledge Women Can Maximize Their Innate Skills to Enhance Their Influence in Business." Lift Leadership, April 2020.

Stanford Graduate School of Business, https://www.gsb.stanford.edu/.

The John Maxwell Team Curriculum, https://johnmaxwellteam.com/john-c-maxwell-certification-program/.

"The Stress Response." ER Services | Disease Prevention and
Healthy Lifestyles. Lumen Learning. https://courses.lu-
menlearning.com/suny-monroecc-hed110//general-adapta-
tion-syndrome/.

Voss, Chris, and Tahl Raz. *Never Split the Difference: Negotiating
As If Your Life Depended On It.* Harper Business, 2016.

Weiss, Leah. *How We Work: Live Your Purpose, Reclaim Your
Sanity, and Embrace the Daily Grind.* New York, NY: Harper
Wave, 2019.

Williamson, Marianne. *A Return to Love: Reflections on the Principles of "A Course in Miracles."* HarperOne, 1996.

"Women CEOs: Catalyst Archives." Catalyst. https://www.cata-
lyst.org/tag/women-ceos/.

RESOURCES

Workplace Harassment/Intimidation Resources

"Harassment." U.S. Equal Employment Opportunity Commission. https://www.eeoc.gov/harassment.

"What Do I Need to Know about… WORKPLACE HARASSMENT." U.S. Department of Labor. https://www.dol.gov/agencies/oasam/centers-offices/civil-rights-center/internal/policies/workplace-harassment/2012.

Workplace Bullying Institute. https://workplacebullying.org.

Sexual Harassment/Abuse Resources

RAINN (Rape, Abuse & Incest National Network). https://www.rainn.org.

Lean In. https://leanin.org.

National Sexual Violence Resource Center (NSVRC). https://www.nsvrc.org.

National Sexual Assault Hotline: 1-800-656-HOPE (4673)

ABOUT THE AUTHOR

Gail Rudolph is an executive coach and trainer with twenty-five years serving in leadership positions across a spectrum of organizations. Gail is a Cialdini Method Certified Trainer (CMCT), one of only thirteen people globally—and one of only two women and the only woman in the United States—to hold this distinction. As a CMCT, she is credentialed to teach Dr. Robert Cialdini's six

powerful, universal *Principles of Persuasion* and provide certification to students as an Ethical Practitioner.

A strategic thinker, Gail helps individuals, teams, and organizations maximize their impact by helping them pivot, change, grow, and move beyond what they've achieved previously. An expert on mindset, interpersonal power, and inclusion and diversity, Gail's mission is to help others become positive "agents of change."

Gail holds a master's degree in Human Services Administration, a Bachelor of Science in Psychology, a Leadership Certification from the Stanford Graduate School of Business and is certified to conduct SHRM-approved diversity training. She is a Value-Based Leadership Expert, Wiley DISC Consultant, and is a Certified Fund Raising Executive (CFRE).

Among her many accomplishments, Gail has been named by *Northwest Business Journal* as one of the "Top 10 Leaders You Should Know." She is an Executive Director on The John Maxwell Team and presently serves on the Maxwell *President's Advisory Council.*

Gail is the CEO and founder of Gail Rudolph Collaborative. She loves bike riding and enjoys cycling in sunny Palo Alto, California.

FREE EXCLUSIVE BONUSES

~~REGULAR PRICE $399~~

- Personal Boundary Inventory
- Access to our Power Up Power Down Exclusive Facebook Community
- Work Place Situations Cheat Sheet
- Power Up Power Down Chart
- What is Power Poster

www.PowerUpPowerDown.com

A free ebook edition is available with the purchase of this book.

To claim your free ebook edition:

1. Visit MorganJamesBOGO.com
2. Sign your name CLEARLY in the space
3. Complete the form and submit a photo of the entire copyright page
4. You or your friend can download the ebook to your preferred device

MorganJames BOGO™

A **FREE** ebook edition is available for you or a friend with the purchase of this print book.

CLEARLY SIGN YOUR NAME ABOVE

Instructions to claim your free ebook edition:
1. Visit MorganJamesBOGO.com
2. Sign your name CLEARLY in the space above
3. Complete the form and submit a photo of this entire page
4. You or your friend can download the ebook to your preferred device

Print & Digital Together Forever.

Snap a photo

Free ebook

Read anywhere

9 781631 95